FROM RED LET'

FORGIVING KIDS

CHALLENGE

A 40-DAY FORGIVENESS ADVENTURE

ZACH AND ALLISON ZEHNDER
with
DOUG PETERSON

Forgiving Challenge Kids
Version 1.0

Copyright 2021
Red Letter Living LLC
www.forgivingchallenge.com
www.redletterchallenge.com
hello@redletterchallenge.com

ALL RIGHTS RESERVED.

No part of this publication may be reproduced, stored, or transmitted in any form or by any means—for example, electronic, photocopy, or recording—without prior written permission. The only exception is brief quotations in printed reviews. Please encourage and participate in doing the right thing.

All Scripture quotations, unless otherwise noted, are taken from THE HOLY BIBLE, NEW INTERNATIONAL VERSION, NIV, Copyright 1973, 1978, 1984, 2011 by Biblica, Inc. Used by permission. All rights reserved worldwide.

Spiritual Gift Test on pages 251-255 used with permission and adapted from www.sdrock.com.

All sources are named. For a full list of source that were used go to www.forgivingchallenge.com/kids/sources.

Cover design and book layout by plainjoestudios.com.

Printed in the United States of America.

#FORGIVINGCHALLENGEKIDS

ACKNOWLEDGMENTS

Thanks first and foremost to Zach Zehnder, the visionary and faithful leader of this project. Your ability to see things before they are there forever inspires me even as I still brace myself when you say, "I have a new idea!"

Doug Peterson, you are a humble and kind man, even though you are a rockstar in the literary world. I still get nervous when I have to send you rough drafts! Thank you for helping us navigate these new waters of drafts, writing, and editing. Your talents are unmatched.

Huge thank you's belong to Maggie VandeVrede and Sydney Kertz for being brilliant and honest editors. It makes all the difference and I respect your work so much.

Much gratitude to Steve and Susan Blount and the entire team at Blount Collective who are dedicated to helping people move to where they believe God intends them to be. It's made a difference in our lives.

I want to dedicate this book to one of my dearest friends, Tabitha Thrasher.

Tabitha, you have had grace, strength, and bravery through difficulty and come through like a diamond in the rough. You are devoted to helping others find freedom in forgiveness. I am incredibly proud of you.

> "Do not be anxious about anything, but in every situation, by prayer and petition, with thanksgiving, present your requests to God. And the peace of God, which transcends all understanding, will guard your hearts and your minds in Christ Jesus." Philippians 4:6-7

— ALLISON ZEHNDER

TABLE OF CONT

ACKNOWLEDGMENTS • • • • • • • 3

YOUR MOUNTAIN IS WAITING • • • 6

THE MOUNTAINS OF REDVALE: PART 1 • • 10

THE WARMUP
DAY 1: THE MESS-UP • • • • • • 16
DAY 2: THE 'FESS-UP • • • • • • 20
DAY 3: THE CLEAN-UP • • • • • 24
DAY 4: THE RISE-UP • • • • • 28
DAY 5: THE STEP-UP • • • • • • 32

THE MESS-UP
THE MOUNTAINS OF REDVALE: PART 2 • 38
DAY 6 • • • • • • • • • • • 48
DAY 7 • • • • • • • • • • • 52
DAY 8 • • • • • • • • • • • 58
DAY 9 • • • • • • • • • • • 62
DAY 10 • • • • • • • • • • 66
DAY 11 • • • • • • • • • • 70
DAY 12 • • • • • • • • • • 74

THE 'FESS-UP
THE MOUNTAINS OF REDVALE: PART 3 • 80
DAY 13 • • • • • • • • • • 90
DAY 14 • • • • • • • • • • 96
DAY 15 • • • • • • • • • • 100
DAY 16 • • • • • • • • • • 106
DAY 17 • • • • • • • • • • 110
DAY 18 • • • • • • • • • • 114
DAY 19 • • • • • • • • • • 118

ENTS

THE CLEAN-UP

THE MOUNTAINS OF REDVALE: PART 4 • 124

DAY 20 • 136

DAY 21 • 140

DAY 22 • 144

DAY 23 • 150

DAY 24 • 154

DAY 25 • 158

DAY 26 • 162

THE RISE-UP

THE MOUNTAINS OF REDVALE: PART 5 • 168

DAY 27 • 180

DAY 28 • 182

DAY 29 • 186

DAY 30 • 190

DAY 31 • 194

DAY 32 • 198

DAY 33 • 202

THE STEP-UP

THE MOUNTAINS OF REDVALE: PART 6 • 208

DAY 34 • 220

DAY 35 • 226

DAY 36 • 230

DAY 37 • 234

DAY 38 • 238

DAY 39 • 242

DAY 40 • 246

WHAT NOW? • 252

THE MOUNTAINS OF REDVALE: PART 7 • 256

ABOUT THE AUTHORS • 268

NOTE TO FACILITATORS • 270

YOUR MOUNTAIN IS WAITING

Edmund Hillary, a famous climber from New Zealand, wanted to be the first man to reach the summit, or the very top, of the tallest mountain in the world—Mount Everest.

Hillary did not get to the top the first time he tried, but he did not give up. After his first unsuccessful climb, he famously said, *"Everest, you beat me the first time, but I'll beat you the next time because you've grown all you are going to grow… but I'm still growing!"*

Then, on May 29, 1953, Edmund Hillary and a Sherpa mountaineer, Tenzing Norgay, became the first climbers to reach the summit of Mount Everest.

Hillary knew that he had a lot of growing to do, just as you too have a lot of growing ahead of you. He accomplished his goal on his second try, but sometimes it can take three, four, or even a hundred tries before you grow strong enough to finish a difficult challenge.

#FORGIVINGCHALLENGEKIDS

In this book, you are going to learn what forgiveness is all about and how to grow into a forgiving person. You will have a chance to study what it means to forgive and what it means to be forgiven. But this will not be something you can master in a day or even 40 days. It is a difficult target and takes lots of work. It might look easy, but it can be very difficult and even feel impossible at times.

In fact, forgiving can feel a lot like climbing a mountain.

From far away, a mountain is beautiful. People admire it and take pictures posing in front of it. From a distance, you can see all the way from the bottom to the top of the mountain in one glance, and you can picture yourself bounding up and down it in no time. But when you get up close to the foot of the mountain, things begin to look differently. From the bottom of the mountain, you may not even be able to see the top, and the steep cliffs can look dangerous and tough. What seemed easy when looked at from far away can feel impossible up close.

When we read about forgiveness in stories or talk about forgiving others, it too can seem like a beautiful thing, like admiring distant peaks. You can see the whole process of forgiveness from the beginning to the end in one glance. It feels easy to tell someone else to forgive. But when you have to get up close to forgiveness, when you have to actually do it yourself, it can feel larger-than-life and difficult. When you have to forgive a really painful hurt or you need to apologize to someone, forgiveness can seem scary and unbearable, like looking up at a mountain from its base.

Forgiveness is difficult, but it is part of our growth as followers of Jesus. We can't ignore forgiveness and expect to understand Jesus because forgiveness is what He's all about.

Over the next 40 days, we will look at the five phases of forgiveness:

1. THE MESS-UP (Sin)
2. THE 'FESS-UP (Confession)
3. THE CLEAN-UP (Absolution)
4. THE RISE-UP (Restoration)
5. THE STEP-UP (Sanctification)

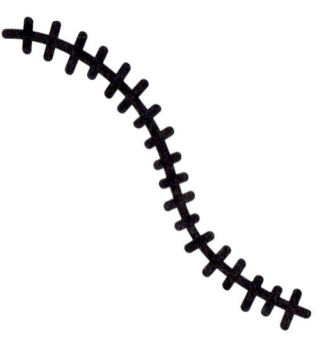

Note that the first 5 letters of the words in parentheses spell SCARS. Old hurts can leave scars on our hearts. When Jesus took our sin to the cross, it left scars on His hands, side, and feet. But His death and resurrection paid for every sin that was ever committed. Jesus is our best example of forgiveness because His forgiveness leaves a bigger mark than your sins could ever leave.

Even after He rose from the dead, Jesus still had scars on His hands from the nails. The disciples could see and touch them. When Jesus wanted to show them His scars, He said: **"Put your finger here, and see my hands; and put out your hand, and place it in my side. Do not disbelieve, but believe." John 20:27 (ESV)**

Forgiveness is not free. It cost Jesus His life. But His scars mean that we are forgiven and that we can be forgiving people too. So load up your backpack, put on your hiking boots, and grab your climbing gear. We've got mountains to climb—and mountains to move.

#FORGIVINGCHALLENGEKIDS

> *"Truly I tell you, if you have faith as small as a mustard seed, you can say to this mountain, 'Move from here to there,' and it will move. Nothing will be impossible for you."* **Matthew 17:20**

THE MOUNTAINS OF REDVALE

In our last two books, *Red Letter Challenge Kids* and *Being Challenge Kids*, you met Aiden, Isabella, and Emily Perez, as they ventured to an incredible land called Redvale. The three Perez kids are back in this book with an all-new adventure that will build on the lessons we learn in *Forgiving Challenge Kids*.

The story begins on page 10 and continues throughout the book.

RED ALERTS!

One of the characters in *The Mountains of Redvale* is Red, a fox who speaks three languages. Scattered throughout the book, you'll find brief Red Alerts from Red the Fox, offering nuggets of information about the Bible.

FIND TEAMMATES

Finally, *Forgiving Challenge Kids* was created to be experienced with others as a family, class, Sunday School, or youth group. We encourage you to find somebody with whom you can embark on this adventure.

Moses spent 40 days on the mountain before God gave him the Ten Commandments. Jesus also spent 40 days in the wilderness before He began His ministry. Let your 40 days begin now!

THE MOUNTAINS OF REDVALE

PART 1

Emily and Aiden Perez thirsted for revenge.

"Something has to be done about Chloe Stallard," Emily told Aiden after a terrible day at school.

"And Frankie Stallard," Aiden said. "Don't forget Frankie."

How could Emily and Aiden forget about either one of them? Chloe was the terror of Emily's class, while her brother Frankie never stopped picking on Aiden. They were classic class bullies—hungry for attention and always suspicious. Just two days earlier, Frankie had called Aiden names and teased him mercilessly for no reason.

On the same day, Chloe poured stinky hand sanitizer in Emily's backpack. Kids could smell Emily all the way down the hall. Every day, Chloe would cut in front of her or trip her in the cafeteria when the teachers weren't looking. It also didn't help that Frankie and Chloe lived just down the street. There was no escaping these two.

"It's time to teach them a lesson," Emily said.

A few days later, their older sister, Isabella, found Emily and Aiden drawing up a plan to get back at Frankie and Chloe. Aiden had a marker in his hand and was sketching out their plan on a large sheet of paper. Isabella couldn't miss the big words, "Operation Slimeball," scrawled on the sheet.

"This isn't the way to respond to bullies," Isabella said, making Emily mad. She hated it when Isabella acted like she was so much better than them.

"What do you suggest?" Aiden said. "Let them walk all over us?"

"**Forgive, and you will be forgiven.** Luke 6:37," Isabella said. Ever since their last visit to the world of Redvale, Isabella had been reading her Bible and quoting Jesus all the time. Emily thought that was cool, except when Isabella quoted Scripture she didn't like to hear.

Isabella was still hassling them on the sunny Saturday morning when they put Operation Slimeball into action.

"**Love your enemies and pray for those who persecute you.** Matthew 5:44," Isabella said, still trying to convince them that this wasn't a good idea. They made their way down the sidewalk running in front of their house.

"I do love my enemies," Emily said. "I love them enough to teach them a lesson they'll never forget."

"Quiet," Aiden said. "Frankie and Chloe dead ahead."

Sure enough, Frankie and Chloe were standing at the end of the block, like menacing dogs. On Saturdays, they would block the sidewalk and force kids to give them things, such as football cards or Pokémon cards, before they let them pass.

"Are you sure we can outrun them?" Emily asked. She was beginning to get nervous.

"I'm sure. You're much faster than Chloe, and I've beaten Frankie in many races."

"All right then. Let the fun begin."

As Aiden and Emily closed in on the bullies, Frankie and Chloe began to chant, "Pay to pass! Pay to pass!"

"You want us to give you things to get by you?" Aiden asked.

"You heard us, sissies!" snapped Frankie. "You know how it works!"

"Oh gee, Aiden, whatever will we do?" Emily said in an over-dramatic voice.

"I don't know what we're going to do, Emily. We don't have any Pokémon cards with us!" Aiden lamented.

"But we do have these!" Emily pulled out a big ball of slime from behind her back.

"You're right!" said Aiden, also pulling out a ball of homemade slime.

#FORGIVINGCHALLENGEKIDS

"Don't do it," Isabella whispered.

The slimeballs looked like snowballs, only gooier and smellier. Aiden had a strong arm in baseball, and Emily was also pretty good at throwing.

"You want payment?" Emily said. "Then take this!"

Winding up like pitchers on a mound, Emily and Aiden let loose.

SPLAT!

Aiden's slimeball hit Frankie squarely in the right shoulder, while Emily's throw nicked Chloe. The two bullies were furious.

"Run!" Isabella shouted. But Aiden and Emily had already wheeled around and were sprinting down the street.

"You can run, but you can't hide!" Frankie hollered, tearing after Aiden.

Up ahead was Verne Park, which was bordered on one side by a thick clump of bushes and some woods. There was a small passage through the bushes, and Aiden and Emily headed straight for it, with Frankie and Chloe not far behind. Isabella also followed.

Crashing through the bushes, Aiden and Emily made sure they steered to the side. Directly on the other side of the bushes was a pit they had dug, about seven feet deep, but they stayed clear of it. Standing around the pit were four other kids from school—other victims of Frankie and Chloe.

"Here's your bucket," said one of the girls, Janelle, handing a pail to Emily.

Each of the kids was armed with a bucket of homemade slime, based on a recipe of Emily's.

"Are you sure this is going to work?" Janelle asked.

"It can't fail. Frankie and Chloe have no idea this pit is here. At least I hope they don't."

"You hope?" Janelle looked like she wanted to turn and run.

"Stay brave," Emily said, clutching her bucket and staring at the bushes. Any second now...

They heard the crashing of bushes as the two bullies powered their way through. Frankie and Chloe were moving so fast that they had no chance to stop when they broke through the bushes and suddenly realized there was no ground beneath their feet.

Emily never forgot the shocked look on their faces as they both tumbled into the pit, landing in a heap at the bottom.

"You want us to pay to pass?" Emily said. "Well, this is our payback!"

As she got ready to heave the bucket of slime onto Frankie and Chloe's heads, she noticed that the other four kids had suddenly become frozen in mid-motion. That's weird. It's like time had stopped, and the other kids had turned into statues. Then the ground suddenly began to shake, rattle, and roll. It couldn't be an earthquake, could it? They lived in Florida, where hurricanes ruled. But not earthquakes.

Isabella appeared next through the bushes, but she knew to stay clear of the pit. "What's going on?" Isabella said, as the shaking of the ground threw her sideways. "What did you two do?"

"I don't know!" Aiden shouted, just before the quake hurled him to the ground.

Frankie and Chloe gazed up from the pit, looking terrified. But then things went from strange to bizarre when the pit deepened and the ground opened up beneath them. They clawed at the side of the pit, trying to climb out, but the soil was being sucked into the hole—and so were they.

Frankie and Chloe disappeared down the hole, vanishing into darkness.

But the earthquake wasn't over yet. The ground gave a mighty jolt, like when a train is starting to leave the station, and Emily lost her footing. She tumbled into the pit. Aiden tried to grab her, but he too lost his balance. And when the earth gave another big jolt, Isabella fell forward as well.

The three Perez kids fell into the pit, amidst cascading soil, which pulled them down, down, down. Then just like that, they were gone.

TO BE CONTINUED ON PAGE 38.

#FORGIVINGCHALLENGEKIDS

THE WARMUP

INTRODUCING...
THE MESS-UP
THE 'FESS-UP
THE CLEAN-UP
THE RISE-UP
THE STEP-UP

DAY 1
THE MESS-UP: SIN

GETTING OFF TRACK

When a climber sets out to climb a mountain, he or she needs loads of supplies. Circle the supplies you may already have at home.

CELL PHONE	WATERPROOF COAT	SUNBLOCK
CARABINERS (CLIPS FOR ROPES)	BACKPACK	GLOVES
CHEST AND WAIST HARNESS	KNIFE	HEADLAMPS
WATER	CLIMBING HELMET	ICE PICK
FIRST-AID KIT	ENERGY BARS	SAFETY ROPE
	CRAMPON	WEATHERPROOF PANTS

These are all important supplies. But even if you have everything you need to be safe on the mountain, none of these things will matter if you don't know where you're headed. You need a GPS or a map to stay on track. Even if you get lost, a map can help you go back and figure out where you went wrong.

It's the same with forgiveness. You need to figure out where you went wrong before you can ask for forgiveness. You need to know what path to take to get right with God or to repair a broken friendship. Take it from King David. God will show you the way forward.

SEARCH ME!

King David was very honest about his sins when writing the Psalms. He understood that if he didn't pinpoint where the trouble started, he wouldn't be able to get right with God. He said it this way:

> **"Search me, O God, and know my heart! Try me and know my thoughts! And see if there be any grievous way in me, and lead me in the way everlasting!" Psalm 139:23-24 (ESV)**

In other words, King David asked God to help him figure out where he had messed up.

When we talk about mess-ups, we're getting into confusing and dangerous territory. You can't fix a mess-up by just telling the other person, "It didn't do much harm" or "Get over it." Mess-ups are a big deal. They can destroy lives. God can help you see where you may have gotten off the path or messed up big time. But God goes even further. He comes to where we are, and He rescues us.

THE RESCUER

In 2002, the famous mountain climber, Dave Hahn, attempted to rescue a climber who had been seriously injured by a falling boulder. To make matters worse, their rescue helicopter crashed, nearly killing him. Did Hahn give up? No, he helped the injured helicopter pilot before deciding to rescue the mountain climber on foot. With the help of several other people, he succeeded.

God is like that. He doesn't give up on us, and He rescues us. As it says in Psalm 40:2, **"He lifted me out of the slimy pit, out of the mud and mire; he set my feet on a rock and gave me a firm place to stand."**

Oftentimes, people think that if they get themselves into a mess, they can get themselves out without any help. The problem with sin is that the harder we try to find our way back on our own, the more lost we become.

For example, you might try to hide your mess-ups. You might hide a vase you broke or a bad grade from your parents. It's normal to try to hide our mess-ups, but it just doesn't work. We need to admit our sins, and we need to look for help. We can't do it all on our own.

Jesus left heaven and came down to earth, with all of its messes. Then He paid the price for our sin by dying in our place. As our rescuer, Jesus invites you to follow Him. But you aren't following Him to save yourself. You follow Him because He saved you. Jesus's death brought us back into a good relationship with our Father. And as forgiven children, we can learn how to forgive others.

It's important to remember three things about forgiveness.

- Forgiveness doesn't mean that what happened didn't matter.
- Forgiveness isn't hiding a mess-up or sweeping a problem under the rug.
- Forgiveness isn't a one-time act.

That is why forgiveness is like a mountain. A mountain can't be climbed in a single step, but a single step starts you on your journey of forgiveness.

#FORGIVINGCHALLENGEKIDS

During the week of the Mess-up, Days 6 to 12, we're going to talk about:

- How all of this hurt started in the world
- Sorting out our hurts
- Hurts on accident vs. hurts on purpose
- Hurts on the inside vs. hurts on the outside
- Hurts from loved ones and hurts in our world

RED ALERT!

People commonly believe that Adam and Eve took a bite out of an apple in the Garden of Eden. But the Bible says they ate "fruit." It doesn't say what kind. Could it have been a banana? Who knows?

DAY 2
THE 'FESS-UP: CONFESSION

THE SAFETY ZONE
Where do you go when you want to feel safe and protected? If you have such a place, this is your safety zone. Draw the place where you feel sheltered and safe.

MY SAFETY ZONE

DO YOU HEAR ME NOW?
Have you ever been talking to someone on the phone when they suddenly start "cutting out" and you can hear only some of their words? The same kind of thing happens when we mess up. Our connection with God starts to cut out like a bad Wi-Fi signal. We don't hear from God clearly.

To solve this problem after a mess-up, we need to 'fess up.

A 'fess-up, or confession, means admitting to your part in the problem—'fessing up to it. However, if you've been hurt in a struggle with a friend or foe, it's tempting to say, "Confessing is just for the people who created the mess. I was hurt, so why do I need to confess? I didn't do anything wrong!"

It's true that in some cases you may not have done anything wrong that you need to confess. But you still need to admit your feelings. You still need to 'fess up and say that you were hurt.

It may be very difficult to 'fess up to our guilty or hurt feelings, but God promises that we won't have to stay hurt and guilty forever. <u>The point of confession is not to remember the sin. It's to receive God's grace.</u>

Everyone messes up. It's what you do *after* the mess-up that makes all the difference. There are lots of ways that kids react when they mess up. Circle all of the reactions below that you have experienced in the past:

- Blame others.
- Ignore the problem.
- Stuff your feelings down deep.
- Cover up the mess.
- Learn to live with the problem.
- Lie about the mess-up.

God tells us that 'fessing up is the best way to deal with sin. **"If we confess our sins, he is faithful and just to forgive us our sins and to cleanse us from all unrighteousness." 1 John 1:9 (ESV)**

When we confess our sin, God repairs the signal. He alone can rightly figure out the cause of the bad connection. He alone knows the proper repair.

CONFESSING TO JESUS

Admitting that someone hurt us may leave us feeling unguarded. It's natural to feel sad when someone hurts us, and it's normal to feel awful when you admit your own fault.

You may not always feel safe when you reveal your feelings to others. You don't need to show those feelings to everyone, but it is very important to have a safe person you can talk to if someone hurt you. They can listen and help you sort out your feelings.

The safest place to confess, the safest place to be, is in the hands of Jesus. His hands have the scars reminding us that He died for us. Jesus can restore the connection. When your phone's connection is being fixed, sometimes you see that spinning buffering wheel going around and around and around and around, driving you crazy. It also takes time to restore our connection with God and with the people we're mad at. Jesus gives you the patience to wait for healing to happen.

There is no need to be afraid of God when we come to Him with our feelings. He always welcomes you with open arms. Copy down the verse 1 John 1:9 on a piece of paper or notecard and put it up in the place you described as your safety zone. During the week of the 'Fess-up, Days 13 to 19, we are going to talk about:

- The fight, flight, or peacemaker responses
- The 3 parts of an apology
- Determining who says what's bad and what's good
- Who we should confess to
- Confessing our sin to God

#FORGIVINGCHALLENGEKIDS

RED ALERT!

God loves a humble heart. In Luke 18:9-14, Jesus tells about a Pharisee who went to the temple and said, "God, I thank you that I am not like other people." Nearby was a tax collector, who said, "God, have mercy on me, a sinner." The tax collector, not the Pharisee, confessed, and he went home "justified" before God. Justified means forgiven.

#FORGIVINGCHALLENGEKIDS

DAY 3

THE CLEAN-UP: ABSOLUTION

CLEANING UP YOUR ACT

The Cub Scouts of America have a pledge called the 'Leave No Trace' Pledge. Here are the six principles of the pledge:

1. KNOW BEFORE YOU GO.
2. CHOOSE THE RIGHT PATH.
3. TRASH YOUR TRASH.
4. BE CAREFUL WITH FIRE.
5. RESPECT WILDLIFE.
6. BE KIND TO OTHER VISITORS.

"Leave No Trace" has become a popular phrase among those who enjoy the outdoors, not just Cub Scouts. Studies have shown that we need to follow these six principles more than ever when we are outdoors. One example of the need can be seen on Mount Everest.

Because of its high altitude, it snows year-round on Mount Everest. Before all of the climbers started coming, the mountain was a land of pure white snow, a spotless landscape. But over the years, the number of climbers has climbed. In 2018, there were 807 summits (climbs) of Everest, plus a whopping 35,000 tourists.

Large numbers of people mean large amounts of trash. What was once a white landscape became a colorful mix of garbage. Shiny metallic wrappers, green tin cans, orange oxygen tanks, yellow laces, and even red socks can be found scattered all over the mountain. Even worse, things that normally decompose (ahem, like going #2) can't break down because it's too cold. So watch where you step! Bad habits, plus the massive number of people, equal a whole lot of mess for the local Nepalese people to deal with.

On the journey of forgiveness, our third step is the Clean-up, or Absolution. To be "absolved" means to be free from guilt and punishment. As you grow, the beautiful life God gave to you will become cluttered with hurts and mess-ups, like the once-pristine slopes of Everest. It's going to happen because we all sin. The Bible says everyone finds themselves in the same boat. **"For everyone has sinned; we all fall short of God's glorious standard." Romans 3:23 (NLT)**

Without a clean-up, we can't move forward. The problem is that the messes are too big for us to clean up on our own. We need help.

THE BIGGEST CLEAN-UP

Jesus came to our world to clean up a mess that was so big, it would make Everest look like an anthill. He did the impossible: He lived a perfect life, and He died and rose again so that our messy lives could get cleaned up.

As Psalm 51:7 says, **"Cleanse me with hyssop, and I will be clean; wash me, and I will be whiter than snow."**

Jesus can take a giant mess and make us as clean as a mountain of pure white snow. He is able to "leave no trace" of our sin. **"As far as the east is from the west, so far has he removed our transgressions from us." Psalm 103:12** "Transgressions" is another word for "sins." And they're gone! It's as if we had a big, smelly junkyard next to our house. But one morning, you look out the window, and it has completely disappeared! In its place is a beautiful playground.

That's kind of like what happens when Jesus removes our sins. He transforms us into something beautiful.

LEAVE-NO-TRACE PLEDGE

Because you know that God has cleaned up your life by forgiving you, it should be easier for you to forgive others. But it can still be tough.

One thing you can do is ask, "How do I make this right?" The goal isn't to make things even and fair, but to show that you are ready to help clean up any mess that you have made. And if you're the one who has been hurt, forgiveness means allowing others to clean up the messes they made in your life.

Take the Leave-No-Trace Pledge for yourself. Pledge to clean up any messes you make in your life. Also, think about how God has made the Leave-No-Trace Pledge for you; He wiped away all of your sins on the cross. So thank Him for it. And while you're at it, make an effort to keep nature just as you found it (or better) when you enjoy the outdoors.

On the following page, sign a pledge to clean up the messes that you make by asking for forgiveness and forgiving others for the messes they make.

#FORGIVINGCHALLENGEKIDS

LEAVE-NO-TRACE PLEDGE

As a child of God, I will do my best to:

- Know right and wrong.
- Try to choose the right path.
- "Own it" when I make a mistake.
- See everyone as a creation of God.
- Be careful with my words.
- Respect other's feelings.

SIGNED:

During the week of the Clean-up, Days 20 to 26, we are going to talk about:

- How to look at both sides of an argument
- What to do when hate keeps us stuck
- Why forgiving is not forgetting
- What happens when God cleans up our mess
- Why forgiveness is not a feeling

DAY 4

THE RISE-UP: RESTORATION

RESTORING RELATIONSHIPS

You learned yesterday that climbers and tourists leave quite a mess on the mountains. Not only does trash ruin the view of a mountain, but it greatly affects the people who call the mountain their home. Therefore, to help keep the mountains and the people who live there safe, the United Nations launched a program calling the years 2021 to 2030 the Decade on Ecosystem Restoration.

Restoration is the act of returning something to a former owner, place, or condition. The United Nations wants to return the mountains to how they used to be before all of the tourists arrived. Similarly, when you restore a broken relationship with a friend or with God, you're restoring things to how they once were.

On the mountain on the next page, do some restoration work of your own:

- Cross out any trash you see on the mountainside.

- Color in some grass for the animals. Many of the mountain people are herders and farmers. If the land becomes overworked, it doesn't have as many nutrients (food for plants) in the soil. Many animals graze on grass, so less grass means less food for animals.

- Draw some crops and rain. Climate change affects the mountain, and landslides and droughts are dangerous for mountain communities.

- Place some trees on the mountain. Trees and plants hold the soil in place and prevent erosion (the movement of soil from one place to another).

A lot of effort has been made to clean up Mount Everest. Since 2014, every climber is required to bring 18 pounds of trash back off the mountain when they climb down. In addition, during the spring of 2018, special clean-up operations removed 8 tons of waste from the mountain. Then, in 2019, the base camp on China's side of the mountain was closed for clean up. People with climbing permits were allowed up the mountain, but visitors and tourists could only get to the areas below the base camp. During the closure, authorities brought 11 tons of waste down from Everest, according to *Recycling* magazine. A group also regularly leads Eco Everest Expeditions, which clean up trash on the mountain.

All of these are efforts to restore Mount Everest, making it as close as possible to the way it used to be. If we let Him, God will lead the restoration efforts in our relationships with other people…and with Him.

RETURN TO THE LORD YOUR GOD

After the Mess-up,
      and the 'Fess-up,
            and the Clean-up,
                  you need to Rise-up.

By forgiving our sin, God doesn't just clean up our mess on the outside. He cleans us from the inside out. He brings us back into relationship with Him and restores us as His children. In Moses's speech to the Israelite people in the Book of Deuteronomy, he spoke about how God restores His people.

"…and when you and your children return to the Lord your God and obey him with all your heart and with all your soul according to everything I command you today, then the Lord your God will restore your fortunes and have compassion on you and gather you again from all the nations where he scattered you. Even if you have been banished to the most distant land under the heavens, from there the Lord your God will gather you and bring you back." Deuteronomy 30:2-4

God's plan from the very beginning was to restore us back to a good relationship with Him and with our world. It's a big task. But God is even bigger.

During the week of the Rise-up, Days 27 to 33, we're going to talk about:

- How forgiveness picks up the pieces and puts things back together
- What it looks like to rise up out of the ashes of sin and be restored
- How to forgive people we don't even know
- What it looks like to rise up after we hurt someone else
- How Jesus rose up from the grave, coming back to life

#FORGIVINGCHALLENGEKIDS

RED ALERT!

When Babylon conquered Jerusalem in 587 B.C., many Israelites were forced into "exile." This means they were forced from their homes and many had to live in Babylon. When the Persians conquered Babylon almost 50 years later, King Cyrus let the Israelites return to the Promised Land. Israel was restored. When we restore a broken friendship, it feels much the same. It feels like coming home.

#FORGIVINGCHALLENGEKIDS

DAY 5

THE STEP-UP: SANCTIFICATION

WORLD RECORDS

If you could beat the world record in something, what would it be?

DATE	YOUR NAME	WORLD RECORD

Edmund Hillary and Tenzig Norgay were the first men to reach the top of Mount Everest. But ever since their amazing accomplishment, many other people have set some incredible records. Here are a few of them:

1965: Nawang Gombu became the first man to climb Everest TWICE.
1975: A British expedition, led by Chris Bongiton, became the first to ascend the southwest face of the mountain.
1975: Junko Tabei became the first woman to reach the summit.
1978: Reinhold Messner and Peter Habeler climbed up the southeast ridge without oxygen tanks.
1998: Tom Whittaker became the first amputee to reach the top of Everest.
2001: Erik Weihenmayer became the first blind man to reach the summit.

All of these accomplishments were made possible because Hillary and Norgay blazed the way, being the first to conquer Mount Everest. With their Everest

Challenge, they inspired others to come after and make their own marks. That is what it means to step up.

By forgiving others, we inspire people to do the same. We encourage others to step up and also learn to forgive. Another way to describe this is "sanctification," which is a fancy way of saying we have been purified and freed from sin.

God doesn't forgive us so we can just sit on a shelf like a statue. He tells us to love others, serve people, and use our talents and be His disciples. (For more on being in a relationship with Jesus or doing what Jesus said, check out *Red Letter Challenge Kids* or *Being Challenge Kids*.) <u>Our forgiveness is an invitation to step up into a life of walking with Jesus and serving others.</u>

Sanctification is the last letter in SCARS. Review the 5 phases of forgiveness by filling in the blanks.

1. THE _____ -UP (S<small>IN</small>)
2. THE _____ -UP (C<small>ONFESSION</small>)
3. THE _____ -UP (A<small>BSOLUTION</small>)
4. THE _____ -UP (R<small>ESTORATION</small>)
5. THE _____ -UP (S<small>ANCTIFICATION</small>)

TAKE THE EVEREST FORGIVENESS CHALLENGE

For a long time, Everest was a challenge for mountaineers who wanted to test their skill. Today, hundreds of climbers go up every year. In fact, there are so many climbers that you can see lines of people leading up the side of the mountain.

You may not be the next climber of Everest, but there will be a time when forgiveness will feel like a bigger challenge than climbing a mountain. You might even think, "But I'm just a kid! Forgiveness is too hard for someone like me."

Kids have thought the same thing about Mount Everest. But a couple of kids proved that you're never too young to take the Everest Challenge. In 2010, Jordan Romero became the youngest male to climb the mountain. He was 13 years old. Then, in 2014, 13-year-old Malavath Poorna became the youngest female to climb the mountain.

If kids can take the Everest Challenge, then you're never too young to take the Forgiveness Challenge. Your summit may be closer than you realize!

When you show forgiveness, you inspire others to do the same. <u>Therefore, when you forgive, you're not just setting yourself free; you're setting up others to be free.</u> You cannot live your true calling without other people; and you can't be around others without learning to practice forgiveness. Forgiveness sets us up for deeper, more trusting relationships.

During the week of the Step-up, Days 34 to 40, we are going to talk about:

- How forgiveness makes us different (in a good way)
- How to be a forgiving person when things get hard
- How forgiveness gives us a new picture of our past hurts
- How forgiveness is only the beginning of a life following Jesus
- How being forgiven means I can help others forgive

#FORGIVINGCHALLENGEKIDS

RED ALERT!

Jesus's ministry lasted only about three and a half years. And yet He changed the world in that short time. We may not change the entire world, but we can still change our own little world—our school or neighborhood. The good news is that you don't need a lot of time to do it.

#FORGIVINGCHALLENGEKIDS

DAYS 6-12

OF THE 40-DAY CHALLENGE

THE MESS-UP:
SIN

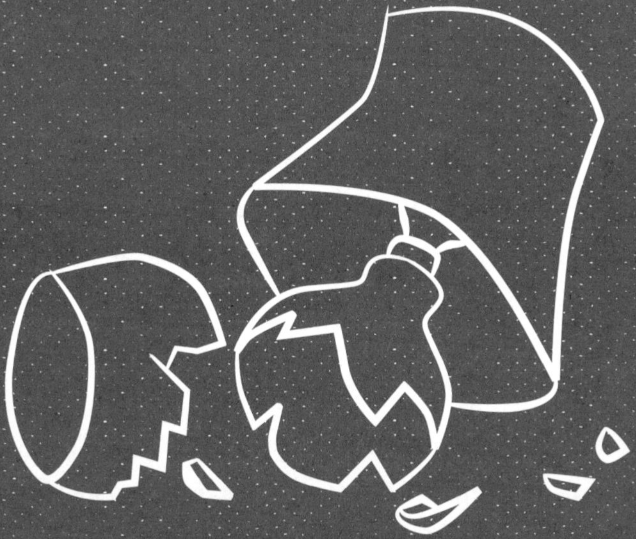

THE MOUNTAINS OF REDVALE

PART 2

Isabella hated roller coasters, but this was so much worse. She was flat on her back, sliding down a deep, dark tunnel at breakneck speed. With roller-coaster rides, at least she knows when it is going to end. She had no idea where this tunnel led. What if it carried them into a pit of lava? Or straight off the edge of a high cliff?

Isabella looked for things to grab as they raced down the dark hole, but all she saw was dirt—fast-flowing soil. The tunnel was steep, and Isabella had the same terrible feeling in the pit of her stomach that she felt on roller-coaster dips.

Was this what they called a bottomless pit? Would she keep sliding forever and ever without end?

Finally, Isabella did the only thing she could think to do in a perilous place. She screamed out a Bible passage: "Rescue me from the mire, do not let me sink! Do not let the depths swallow me up or the pit close its mouth over me!"

As if to answer her plea, the tunnel began to level out. They continued to race at incredible speed, but at least they were no longer plunging straight down. The tunnel twisted sharply to the right as it leveled out some more. Then, miracle of miracles, they began to slow down. The soil still flowed beneath her back, but not as quickly.

"I see a light!" Emily shouted, her voice echoing off of the tunnel walls.

She was right. This tunnel did have an end. But they were still moving fast enough that it would be hard to stop if the tunnel carried them to the edge of a cliff. One by one, the three Perez kids shot out of the tunnel into the blazing sunlight. And one by one, the kids came crashing into a clump of bushes.

#FORGIVINGCHALLENGEKIDS

"Oomph!" Isabella slammed into Emily, who had just smashed into Aiden, who had crashed into the bushes. They wound up in a tangle of arms and legs.

"Get off of me!" Emily shouted, pinching Isabella in the leg.

"Hey! Quit it!" Isabella tried to untangle her right leg, but she hit Aiden in the face by mistake.

"Ow! What did you do that for?" Aiden moaned, untangling himself and holding a hand to his mouth. It looked like his lip was bleeding. Isabella started to apologize, but she quickly changed her mind. Aiden and Emily had gotten her into this mess. They were the ones who needed to apologize to her!

"Serves you right, after what you just did," Isabella snapped.

"What are you talking about?" Aiden said.

"You and Emily caused all of this! That's what I mean!"

Emily shot to her feet. "What did I do? I didn't make the ground open up beneath us!"

"Oh, you didn't, did you? You and Aiden dug that pit!"

Aiden was next on his feet, spitting mad. "We may have dug the pit, but we didn't cause the earthquake! You think we have that kind of power?"

"Maybe you didn't do it on purpose, but if you hadn't created that pit, we wouldn't be in this mess! I told you not to do it! I told you!" As Isabella rose to her feet, she felt aches in her back and right knee. Her left wrist also hurt, and she hoped she hadn't sprained it.

"All I know is that you can't blame me," Emily said, pointing a finger at Aiden. "Digging the pit was Aiden's idea!"

Aiden wheeled around and pointed back at Emily. It looked like they were about to start sword fighting with their pointed fingers. "But getting revenge on Frankie and Chloe was your idea, Emily! So it's your fault!"

"Getting revenge wasn't the problem. Digging that pit was the problem. This is your fault, Aiden!"

"It's both of your faults!" Isabella shouted, pointing two fingers, one at Aiden and the other at Emily. It was the craziest sight, Emily pointing at Aiden, Aiden pointing at Emily, and Isabella pointing at both of them. But even crazier was what happened next. As the three siblings stood there, glaring and pointing at one another, a butterfly suddenly fluttered into view. It was a monarch butterfly, with a striking orange color, like a living stained-glass window.

Aiden, Emily, and Isabella went stone quiet. With fingers still pointed, they stared in amazement as the butterfly flew among them and gently landed on the very tip of Emily's finger.

"Will you look at that?" Aiden said.

"Ssshh," said Isabella. "You'll scare it away."

When Isabella extended her hand, the butterfly flitted away from Emily and landed on her finger. It tickled her fingertip. Then Aiden extended his hand, and the monarch rose into the air, gently landing on his finger. All anger was gone in that moment. It was replaced by wonder.

"It's about time you all arrived," came a voice from behind. A familiar voice. "I've been wondering when you would show up."

The butterfly fluttered away as the three kids turned to see their old friend, Red the Fox. A talking fox. He came bounding around a big boulder, all smiles. Behind him was another good friend, Malachi. His beard seemed to be even longer since the last time they had seen him. As usual, he carried a wooden staff and was dressed like a person from the Bible, except for his shoes. Normally, he wore gym shoes, but today he had on hiking boots.

Malachi must've seen where they were staring because he lifted one boot and said, "We've got a lot of climbing ahead of us. These grip the ground better than gym shoes."

"Climbing?" Isabella said.

"Look around. Mountains everywhere. And where there are mountains, there's climbing."

#FORGIVINGCHALLENGEKIDS

Isabella, Aiden, and Emily had been so busy arguing that they hadn't even checked out where they had wound up. Malachi was right. They were in the midst of the mountains of Redvale—the Crimson Mountains. They appeared to be part of the way up an especially ominous-looking mountain, with smoke rising from its top.

"Is that…?"

"It is," came another familiar voice. "It's a volcano."

The Perez kids turned to face a donkey coming up the path. It was their old friend, Balthazar, the donkey they had met during their first trip to Redvale. They rushed to the donkey's side and wrapped him in warm hugs.

Then Isabella pulled back, as it dawned on her what Balthazar just said. "Did you say we're standing on the side of volcano?"

"We better get down from here before it blows its lid," said Aiden.

But as the three Perez kids began to move, Malachi, Red, and Balthazar didn't budge.

"What are you waiting for?" Emily asked.

"Do you want to tell them, or should I?" asked Red, looking over at Malachi and Balthazar.

"Malachi, you're better at explaining these things," said Balthazar.

"What things?" asked Emily.

"Take a seat on those stones," Malachi said, motioning to several small boulders. As the kids settled in, Malachi looked up at the top of the volcano. "Redvale is under attack again by the Destroyers. They've triggered this volcano, and if something isn't done, all of the towns for miles around will be destroyed."

Isabella had a sudden sinking feeling. Why couldn't they ever come to Redvale for a peaceful visit? Why did there always have to be trouble?

"But it's not just any old volcano," said Malachi. "This one doesn't spew lava."

"No lava? That's a good thing, isn't it?" said Aiden.

"Not really," said Red, leaping up onto a rock. "It spews SLIME!"

Isabella looked over at Emily. "You mean like the slime that Emily and Aiden wanted to hurl on Frankie and Chloe?"

"Quiet! They don't need to know about that," Emily said.

"Oh, but we already do," said Balthazar. "We also know that Frankie and Chloe are trapped inside Mount Goel."

"Mount Goel?"

"That's the name of this volcano."

Isabella's mouth went very, very dry. She was terrified about what Malachi might say next.

"Frankie and Chloe need to be rescued," he said.

Yup. That's what she was afraid he would say.

Emily shot to her feet. "You want us to risk our lives for Frankie and Chloe? I'm sorry. That's not going to happen."

"What's the fastest way down from this mountain?" Aiden said, also leaping to his feet.

"Guys. Let's listen to what Malachi has to say," said Isabella.

"No way!" Emily shouted. She and Aiden spotted a narrow pathway leading downward and were already heading for it.

"Come back!" Isabella pleaded.

"So long! Frankie and Chloe are the bad guys! Why would we want to rescue bad guys?" said Aiden.

Isabella looked over at Malachi, Red, and Balthazar. "Can't you do something to stop them from leaving?"

Malachi and Balthazar said nothing, but Red leaped down from the rock. "Well I don't know about the rest of you, but I'm going to stop them."

Then the little red fox took off down the path, as the side of the mountain began to quake. Isabella stared up at the peak of Mount Goel and saw slime spouting from the top. It smelled to high heavens.

#FORGIVINGCHALLENGEKIDS

NOWHERE TO RUN

Aiden and Emily stopped to look up at the volcano. The ground shook, and green slime shot into the air from the top of the mountain. Then, just as suddenly as the shaking began, it stopped. It was not a full-blown eruption, but who knew when this volcano would explode? They needed to get down the mountain as soon as they could, Aiden thought.

"Hold on, you guys!" shouted Red, bounding right behind him. "You've got to do as Malachi says!"

"No we don't," said Aiden, rushing down the path and feeling a growing outrage. He felt like he too was about to erupt. How dare Malachi ask them to rescue Frankie and Chloe! Rescue the two kids who tormented them every day at school?

"We can't just leave them trapped inside the volcano!" Red said, coming up alongside them.

"Then why don't you, Malachi, Isabella, and Balthazar save them?" Emily said. "Just don't ask us."

"It isn't our fault they're trapped inside that volcano," Aiden added.

"That's right," Emily said, stomping heavily. "It wasn't our fault!"

"But you dug the pit!" Red said.

"Yes, we dug the pit, but we couldn't know it would suck them into a volcano!"

Ignoring Red's pleas, the two of them continued down the path, which zigzagged down the mountain in a series of switchbacks. Aiden covered his nose because the slimy smell floating down from the mountain was sickening.

As the mountain rumbled and shook once again, Aiden and Emily picked up speed, with Red still at their side. Leaping over stones, Aiden's heart began to beat wildly. The path in front of them suddenly seemed to move, as if it were alive, and the ground vibrated. Then something huge began to rise from the ground. It looked like a gigantic boulder was pushing out of the soil, directly in their path.

"Turn! Run!" Emily said.

"I think it's a cave whale!" Aiden shouted, watching the stone creature rise from the ground. "Do you think it could be Bob?"

They had met Bob the Cave Whale during their first trip to Redvale. And in case you don't know your Redvale creatures, a cave whale is just what it sounds like. It's a cave that looks like a whale and swims beneath the soil.

"I'm not going to wait to find out if its Bob!" Emily shouted. "Run!"

As Aiden turned to flee, he saw two eyes on the sides of the stone whale. A huge, gaping mouth opened wide like a yawning cave.

Please be Bob. Please be Bob, Aiden prayed as he strained to run back up the mountainside to get away from the creature. Then he sensed a darkness coming over him like a cloak, and he looked over his shoulder to see the cave whale's wide-open mouth only a few feet behind them. He felt the cool air of a cave as the whale gulped them up. The cave whale's mouth snapped shut, and everything went totally and completely and utterly dark.

IN THE BELLY OF THE WHALE

During their first visit to Redvale, Isabella and Red were the ones swallowed by Bob the Cave Whale. So this was a new experience for Emily and Aiden. They slid down a slippery surface, landing in what must be the whale's stomach.

Emily picked herself up and shouted at the cave roof. "Bob! Is that you, Bob?"

"Save your breath," came a voice from the dark. "It's not easy for a cave whale to have a conversation with people in his stomach."

"Who said that?" Emily asked, staring into the dark.

"Permit me to introduce myself. My name is Rockette Boulder, the daughter of Orville Boulder, son of Homer Boulder, son of Mookie Boulder, son of Leo Boulder, son of…"

"I know who you are!" chirped Red, leaping out of the darkness and into view. "It's good to see you again, Rockette!"

"Well if it isn't my old friend Red," said the rock, with a grin that split the

#FORGIVINGCHALLENGEKIDS

stone. Emily stood staring in amazement.

"Did that rock just talk to us?" she asked.

"Of course!" said Rockette. "Haven't you been to Redvale enough times to realize that strange things happen a lot?"

The rock was right about that.

"We met Rockette and her friends the last time we were inside Bob's belly," Red explained.

"So this is Bob's belly then?" Emily said. "That's a relief."

"But why did Bob swallow us?" Aiden asked.

"Because you're running in the wrong direction," said Rockette. "If you haven't noticed, whales have a way of swallowing people who go the wrong way. Do you remember good old Jonah?"

"Of course," said Emily.

"Do you remember what he was running from?"

"Remind me."

"God asked Jonah to tell the people of Nineveh to repent. But Jonah hated the Ninevites. He didn't want them to repent and be forgiven. So he fled!"

"Before he could flee too far, he was swallowed by a big fish," Red added. "He was in the belly of the beast for three days."

"Three days! We don't have to be in here that long, do we?" asked Aiden.

"Maybe. Maybe not," said Rockette. "It depends on your heart. Will your heart be hard, or will it be soft?"

"Isn't your heart hard?" Emily asked Rockette.

"Yeah, but I'm a rock. My heart is supposed to be hard. But your heart is supposed to be soft. You're supposed to care for others."

"Even for Frankie and Chloe?" Aiden asked.

"*Especially* for Frankie and Chloe."

Emily sat down on a rock—and then just as quickly jumped up. "Sorry," she said to the stone, who smiled back at her.

"No worries. That happens all the time."

THE MOUNTAINS OF REDVALE • 45

"You have to face the truth," said Rockette. "You messed up. The first step to forgiveness is to admit when you mess up."

"Do you really think if we hadn't dug that pit, then Frankie and Chloe wouldn't be trapped in the volcano?" Aiden asked.

"I'm sorry to say, but it's true," said Rockette. "Your pit sucked them into Mount Goel. So it's up to you two to help rescue them."

"If I recall," said Red, "Jonah called out to the Lord when he was inside that big fish. He said, 'To the roots of the mountains I sank down; the earth beneath me barred me in forever. But you, Lord my God, brought my life up from the pit.'"

"Your mission is to travel to the roots of the mountain," Rockette said. "Then the Lord will bring you up from the pit. He will also bring Frankie and Chloe up from the pit."

When Emily heard those words, an ornery, stubborn feeling came over her. She didn't want the Lord to bring Frankie and Chloe up from the pit. She didn't want to see them forgiven. Those two bullies needed to suffer!

Was her heart becoming hard? She put a hand to her chest, as if she were afraid she was turning to stone. She sighed as she felt the thump of her heartbeat.

"I don't like this," Aiden said. "I don't like this one bit."

"God doesn't ask you to like it," Red said. "But He does ask you to do it."

Emily rapped on the cave wall a couple of times and shouted, "All right, Bob! We'll do it. We'll help rescue those two horrible, terrible, lousy, stinking kids! But we're not going to like one minute of it!"

"Do you think he could hear that?" Aiden asked, just before a big jolt hurled him to the ground. Bob the Cave Whale was on the move again.

"I think he heard you, so hold on! This is my favorite part!" Rockette shouted as she rolled from one side of the cave to the other, like a pinball.

Emily, Aiden, and Red also tumbled about as Bob the Cave Whale carried them up the side of the mountain. They could hear the crunch of splitting rock as he moved. They also heard…

BURPPPP!

#FORGIVINGCHALLENGEKIDS

The cave whale let loose with a stone-shattering burp, and a mighty wind slammed them from behind, hurling them forward. The whale's mouth opened wide, and they went flying out into the sunlight.

They landed at the feet of Malachi, Isabella, and Balthazar.

"Oh, my aching back," Emily said, rising from the ground. "Couldn't Bob belch in a more gentle way?"

"Sorry," said Bob. "Can you forgive me?"

Rubbing her sore back, Emily turned to face her old friend. She could see sadness in the eyes of Bob the Cave Whale, and Emily felt bad for getting angry.

"Of course I forgive you!" she shouted, running up to Bob and giving him a hug—although it's kind of difficult to wrap your arms around a cave whale.

Then Emily looked up at the top of Mount Goel, which was beginning to rumble again. "What are we waiting for?" she said. "We have a mountain to climb."

TO BE CONTINUED ON PAGE 80.

DAY 6

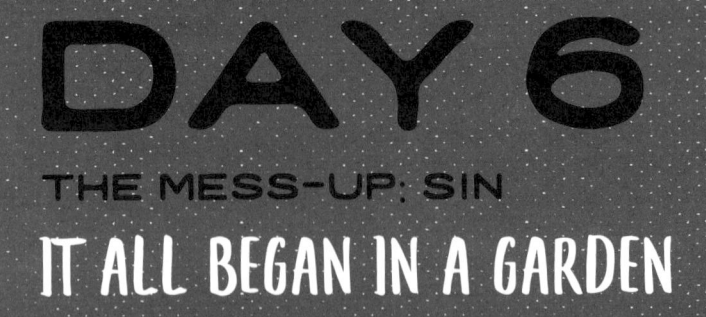

THE MESS-UP: SIN

IT ALL BEGAN IN A GARDEN

HOW DID ALL OF THIS HURT START?

A monarch butterfly can fly about one mile in 11 minutes, a little slower than what the average human can run. But a monarch can do something no human can. Monarch butterflies fly thousands of miles every single year to warmer climates. (Okay, okay, some humans fly south in the winter too, but they do it in planes, not with wings.) The eastern population of monarchs migrates 4,830 miles (7,773 kilometers) across the ocean to Mexico in winter.

God made this world in a wonderful and interwoven design. When you look at our world and examine the different ways that animals live, you see evidence of a Grand Creator. Someone had a master plan when this world was made. It didn't just happen by chance.

But something also happened to mess up this world. That something is called sin. Sin happens any time the world and people don't act the way God made them to. The Bible tells us that there were two humans called Adam and Eve who chose to break the one rule that God set for them: "Don't eat from the Tree of the Knowledge of Good and Evil." They wanted to be like God by making their own rules and being their own boss.

When sin came into the world, God's perfect design began to unravel. God said to Adam and Eve, **"…you'll be working in pain all your life long. The ground will sprout thorns and weeds, you'll get your food the hard way, planting and tilling and harvesting, sweating in the fields from dawn to dusk." Genesis 3: 17b-18 (The Message)**

Because of Adam and Eve's choice, God warned them that things would not always work the way they used to. Life will often be hard. Hurts on the outside will happen in nature, such as weeds, decay, and death. There will also be hurts on the inside, such as jealousy, sadness, and fury.

It didn't take long for sin to spread across the world, like weeds. Adam and Eve had two sons named Cain and Abel, and in a jealous rage Cain killed his brother. It was the first murder in history.

Even though His perfect world was getting messed up, God did not give up on us. He sent His son Jesus to begin the process of weaving this world back together. Jesus told many people, **"The Kingdom of God is at hand!"** This means that God is still the ruler of the world, and He's working to fix everything that is ruined.

Only Jesus can take your hurts and fix what was broken. If He can design tiny butterflies to fly thousands of miles, He can fix what is broken no matter how messed up it is.

CHALLENGE

God made monarch butterflies with the instinct to fly thousands of miles to nest. He made your body to work in amazing ways too. A workout app found that the average adult can run a mile in 9 minutes and 48 seconds, according to an August 2019 article in *Runner's World*.

Time how fast you can run. Go out on your sidewalk, a park, or an open track and ask a friend or parent to time you running for 200 meters. Use the stopwatch on the clock app on your phone.

As you're running, think about how you feel when you start and how you feel as you're running. As you begin to breathe harder, remember that even though sin came into the world, even though things are difficult (such as running very fast for 200 meters), God still is in control.

Below, record how fast you ran in seconds.

200 METERS IN _____ SECONDS

Next, figure out what your time would be if you could keep running at that pace for an entire mile.

_____ X 8 = _____ SECONDS PER MILE.
(YOUR TIME)

Finally, calculate your time in miles per hour.

_____ /60 = _____ MINUTES PER MILE
(YOUR TIME IN SECONDS PER MILE)

Do you think you could keep up that pace for, oh, let's say 5,000 miles?!

#FORGIVINGCHALLENGEKIDS

Finally, dig a little deeper by answering these questions:

How is your body and the world different because of sin?

_____

_____

_____

How does it feel to know that God is in control and will never give up on His creation?

_____

_____

_____

RED ALERT!

The word "sin" comes from an old archery word that means "to miss the mark." If you don't hit the bullseye on a target, then you "miss the mark." That's what sin is like. It means that even when we aim to do right, we often miss our target. But the Good News is that Jesus still forgives us. We're not perfect, but our Heavenly Father is. He loves us with perfect love.

DAY 7
THE MESS-UP: SIN
BUMPS, STINGS, AND CUTS

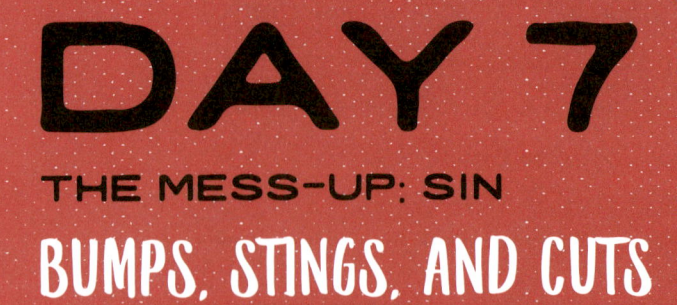

SORTING OUR HURTS

Yesterday we learned that sin came into the world through Adam and Eve when they disobeyed God. Ever since then, the disobedience has spread. As a result, we all have hurts and pains that we must forgive.

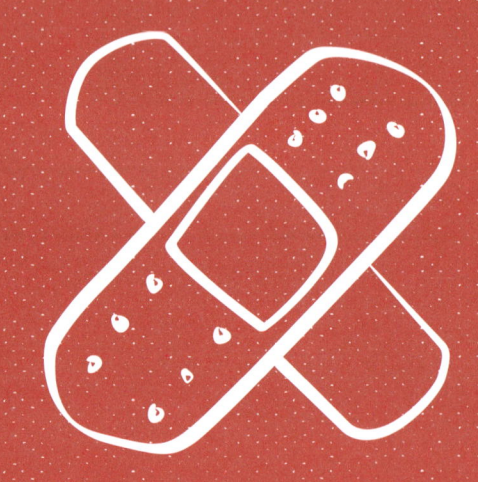

However, not every hurt and pain in your life needs forgiveness. The first step in forgiveness is learning to sort out our hurts and decide which ones need forgiveness. We'll call those different hurts "bumps, stings, and deep cuts."

A BUMP

Jake really loved Snickers candy bars and was hoping to get a bunch when he went trick-or-treating. But as Jake sorted out his candy, he was disappointed to discover that he got only one Snickers. He was frustrated, but no one was at fault for what happened. So Jake didn't need to forgive anyone. His disappointment was a "bump."

Instead of feeling sad, he could look at all of the other treats and goodies that he had gotten. This was his biggest pile yet, so he had a lot to be thankful about.

>> What is something that was a little disappointing to you but was no one's fault? It just happened. That could be a bump.

A STING

Nora came home one day feeling sad. Her classmates didn't notice that she had worn brand-new shoes. Also, her friend Lucy didn't share her fruit snacks, even though they were Nora's favorite, and no one asked her how her injured dog, Murphy, was doing.

However…Nora hadn't told anyone about her new shoes or shared that Murphy had been hurt by falling in a hole. As for Lucy, she had completely forgotten that fruit snacks were Nora's favorite.

Nora's feelings were stung. In this case, some stings will need to be forgiven, but some won't.

Sometimes we want people to read our minds and know what we are thinking. But if we don't talk about our feelings, how can people figure out what is going on in our lives? We should be able to forgive people for things they didn't mean to do—or things they couldn't even know. How were Nora's friends to know she was upset about her dog? They didn't even know her dog was hurt!

>> What is something that hurt for a little while, but you were able to forgive and move past it and still have a relationship with the person? That might be a sting.

DEEP CUTS

Ava was so excited. Her last virtual class had just ended, and finally she was able to go outside. She ran into the garage, only to find her bicycle gone! After searching all over the place, her parents called the police and reported a missing bike. Later, they found it at a neighbor's place a few houses down. An older boy had taken it, ripped off the white wicker basket and shiny bell, and ridden it through mud while doing stunts. The bike was ruined, and the boy's family had no money to fix or replace it.

Ava was heartbroken. She wondered if the boy had been watching her play in the backyard just before he stole the bike. She didn't feel safe leaving anything in the garage anymore. Ava's heart had been cut deeply. She would need forgiveness to help her heal.

> What is something that happened to you that you still think about? It still hurts when you remember it, and you think about it whenever you see the person who caused the hurt. That might be a deep cut.

BY HIS WOUNDS...

No one is able to tell you which hurts will be a bump, sting, or deep cut. It is up to you to discover that. Knowing when someone has caused a bump or sting or deep cut will help you decide when you need to forgive.

Throughout the week of the Mess-up, you're going to study the hurts you have caused, as well as the ones you have received from others. As you think about them, keep in mind the bump, the sting, and the deep cut.

#FORGIVINGCHALLENGEKIDS

If you gather every hurt into a pile and then try to throw forgiveness over the whole thing like a blanket, you won't know which hurts are deep wounds and which hurts can be easily ignored. You need to sort them. It also may be tempting to stuff everything down deep and pretend they never happened. But that will not work because sin needs to be dealt with.

Romans 6:23 says, **"For the wages of sin is death, but the free gift of God is eternal life in Christ Jesus our Lord." (ESV)** Through sin, death and pain entered the world, and it continues to create trouble. Sin is like a monster on the loose, and you wouldn't ignore a monster if it was tearing apart your house, would you?

However, we cannot heal the deep cuts of sin on our own power. Only Jesus can save us. The gift of eternal life is free for us, but it cost Jesus His life. When Jesus died for our sins, He received very deep cuts that left scars on His body:

- He had nails in His hands and feet.
- He had a crown of thorns on His head.
- He had deep slashes on His back from a whip.
- He was pierced in His side by a spear.

Jesus died on the cross from those deep cuts. But after three days, He rose again and defeated death. He rose to give us new life. Jesus took deep cuts for us so that we could live as healed and brand-new people.

Long before Jesus was born, Isaiah prophesied what would happen to Him. As Isaiah 53:5b says, **"...by his wounds we are healed."**

CHALLENGE

Think about some hurts that you have caused or received in the past. Sort them out in the chart below.

BUMPS	STINGS	DEEP CUTS

#FORGIVINGCHALLENGEKIDS

RED ALERT!

There were four types of crosses used for crucifixions. One was shaped like an X, another looked like a plus sign, and a third looked like a T, with the crossbeam across the top. The one we're most familiar with is called the Latin cross. The crossbeam is positioned part of the way down the upright beam, like a small "t." All of them were terrible punishments. Jesus loved us deeply to suffer for our sake.

#FORGIVINGCHALLENGEKIDS

DAY 8

THE MESS-UP: SIN
HURTS ON THE INSIDE AND OUTSIDE

SCAR STORIES

Scars tell a story. Think of a scar you have. How did you get it? Draw it in on the figure below. Then write or draw about how you got that scar.

We can see the scars on the outside of our bodies, but how can you tell if you have a "deep cut" on the inside? Here are three ways you might be able to tell if you have a sting or deep cut that needs healing.

1. YOU TRY TO FAKE YOUR FEELINGS OR PRETEND SOMETHING DIDN'T HURT YOU.

Carlee didn't get invited to the birthday party for a girl in her class. Even though she was hurt and felt left out, she pretended that she didn't care.

2. YOU HAVE A RECURRING PAINFUL MEMORY THAT COMES BACK TO HAUNT YOU.

Jordan still remembers what it felt like when his uncle yelled at him. Jordan didn't mean to bounce his ball near a candle, but his uncle hollered at him and took his ball away. Now, every time Jordan is around his uncle, he remembers his harsh words.

3. YOU DON'T FEEL SAFE AROUND A PERSON, PLACE, OR ACTIVITY BECAUSE OF WHAT HAPPENED.

Sam used to love soccer. He wasn't the best kid on the team, but he had so much fun with his teammates learning the game. After a kid on the team called him "giraffe" because of his long legs, Sam became self-conscious. The uniform looked shorter on his long legs than the other kids' uniforms, and Sam was embarrassed to wear it.

LOOKING AT THE HEART

When Israel was looking for someone to replace King Saul, most people overlooked David. After all, wasn't David the youngest and shortest of the brothers? But the prophet Samuel told the people that God can see both the outside and the inside of us.

When Samuel looked at an older, taller son, the Lord told him, **"Do not consider his appearance or his height, for I have rejected him. The Lord does not look at the things people look at. People look at the outward appearance, but the Lord looks at the heart." 1 Samuel 16:7**

Because God looks at the heart, He can see the cuts on both the inside and outside. He cares about our hurts and wants us to be healed and forgiven. Jesus rescues us, so that we can feel safe. Forgiveness is a way of saying, "I'm not going to let this person continue to hurt me."

Jesus's scars can cover any of our scars, both inside and outside. He sees your heart, and He heals your heart.

RED ALERT!

When we're hurt on the outside, we often bleed. Blood is also a powerful symbol of sacrificial love. Lambs gave their lives so blood could be put on the doorways of the Israelites in Egypt, protecting them from death. Jesus, the Lamb of God, shed His blood so we too could be protected from death. Through Him, we have eternal life.

CHALLENGE

Sort through the following hurts. Put a checkmark next to things that hurt on the outside and things that hurt on the inside. Some of these things can be both outside and inside hurts. At the end of the list, add your own hurts.

	OUTSIDE HURTS	INSIDE HURTS
Someone ignores you.	☐	☐
You get a paper cut.	☐	☐
Someone calls you a name.	☐	☐
Someone hits you.	☐	☐
Someone steals your toy.	☐	☐
You stub your toe.	☐	☐
You fall and skin your knee.	☐	☐
Someone trips you on purpose.	☐	☐

OTHER HURTS:

_____	☐	☐
_____	☐	☐
_____	☐	☐

THE MESS-UP

DAY 9

THE MESS-UP: SIN
HURTS ON ACCIDENT

HAPPY BIRTHDAY!

Decorate the birthday cake below. How many candles will you have on your next birthday cake? Add those to the picture.

THE FROZEN DISASTER

Bella wanted so badly to have an ice cream cake for her birthday. But because her family didn't have much money, Bella's mom found she could make a cake out of ice cream sandwiches and whipped cream, rather than buying one at the store. Her mom even added sprinkles and gumballs all around the edges.

Bella couldn't wait for everyone to see her beautiful cake.

But when Bella's mom brought out the cake, something was terribly wrong. Bella's mom mistakenly put the finished ice cream cake in the refrigerator instead of the freezer. As a result, the ice cream didn't stay frozen, and the neatly stacked ice cream sandwiches had begun to melt. The cake no longer looked like a cake. It looked like a mountain of brown and white mush.

The cake was too soft to insert candles, so everyone sang to Bella—but she had no candles to blow out. Bella didn't want her mom to know how disappointed she was, so she put on a fake smile and pretended to laugh at the cake as a lump formed in her throat.

Bella's birthday wish for an ice cream cake didn't come true. Even though her mom had caused a hurt, it was by accident. Nevertheless, Bella still needed to forgive the "sting" her mom had caused.

SLEEPING ON THE JOB

Have you ever felt like Bella? Has someone who loves you ever hurt you by accident or without knowing it?

Perhaps a teacher lost a project you worked on so hard, or maybe your brother dropped and broke something that belonged to you. Even if we know they didn't mean to hurt us, it still stings.

Jesus's very best friends, the disciples, hurt Him without realizing it. One night, Jesus went to the Garden of Gethsemane to pray. He asked His disciples to come with Him and pray for Him while He went off alone. But one by one they dozed off. When Jesus came back, they were all fast asleep.

Jesus was hurt by this. When He woke them, He asked Peter, **"Can't you stick it out with me a single hour? Stay alert; be in prayer so you don't wander into temptation without even knowing you're in danger." Mark 14:37 (The Message)**

The same thing happened two more times throughout the night! The disciples tried to keep their eyes open, but they just couldn't stay awake. The Bible says their eyelids were heavy. The disciples didn't mean to hurt Jesus; they fell asleep by accident.

Has someone ever told you, "But it was just an accident!" when they hurt you? Did that make it any better? Remember… You do not have to prove that someone meant to hurt you before you can forgive.

OTHER UNFAIR HURTS

Getting hurt "by accident" just doesn't seem fair. But we all experience many types of unfair hurts. Here are a few more examples.

1. SOMEONE WAS GETTING BACK AT YOU FOR SOMETHING YOU DIDN'T DO.

Connor yelled at his brother for taking his clothes, only to find out later that their babysitter accidentally switched the laundry. His anger was unfair.

2. SOMETIMES PEOPLE'S OWN HURTS SPILL ONTO OTHERS.

Tim bragged about his accomplishments and always tried to one-up his friend Cayden. Cayden didn't realize that Tim's dad was always putting him down and making fun of him. Tim wanted his dad's approval, and being better than Cayden made Tim feel better about himself.

#FORGIVINGCHALLENGEKIDS

3. SOME PEOPLE DO BAD THINGS, EVEN THOUGH THEY THINK THEY'RE MAKING A GOOD CHOICE.

Mia didn't tell her parents that her sister Charlotte bought an app on her iPad without asking. She wanted to keep the peace and didn't want to get Charlotte in trouble. However, their parents later learned that Charlotte had over $300 worth of charges on this app. Mia didn't want to be a tattle-tale, but instead a lot of trouble resulted for Charlotte and their parents.

CHALLENGE

Because of sin, we all face times when someone hurts us "by accident." Draw or write about a time you did something that you never meant to do. It's okay to say it was an accident. But even if you didn't mean to do it, you still need to apologize and listen to the other person.

THE BIG ACCIDENT

DAY 10

THE MESS-UP: SIN
HURTS ON PURPOSE

THE HIDING PLACE

Corrie ten Boom was a courageous Dutch woman who was sent to a concentration camp for hiding Jews during World War II. The German Nazis were hunting Jews and sending them to death camps.

Corrie survived the death camp, but her precious sister Betsie did not. Despite the suffering, when the war ended Corrie went to Germany in 1947 with a message of forgiveness. "When we confess our sins," she told the people in a German church one day, "God casts them into the deepest ocean, gone forever."

After her talk, a German man approached. Corrie was horrified. She recognized this man as one of the brutal guards at her concentration camp. He didn't recognize her, but he told her he had been a guard at one of these evil camps. He also said he'd become a Christian after the war and knew that God had forgiven him for the cruel things he did. Then he held out his hand and said the words that Corrie most feared: "Will you forgive me?"

Corrie wasn't sure she could.

DOUBLE FORGIVING

Yesterday we talked about hurts on accident. Today we are talking about hurts on purpose. These are hurts caused by people who had time to think and plan out their actions. Their plan was to cause pain. That guard was well aware of the evil he was doing.

When someone hurts us on purpose, it means we may have to do some double forgiving. We have to forgive the deep cut that was caused, and we have to forgive the meanness behind the hurt.

In other words, the purpose behind the person's actions can affect our feelings.

AMAZING GRACE

The Roman soldiers treated Jesus in brutal ways—whipping Him, pushing a crown of thorns on His head, making fun of Him, and nailing Him to the cross. But note what Jesus said while hanging on the cross. He said, **"Father, forgive them; they don't know what they're doing." Luke 23:34 (The Message)**

Wow! Jesus forgave the soldiers who killed Him. The Roman soldiers probably thought they were just doing their job, ridding the world of a criminal. But as horrible as their actions were, it didn't stop Jesus from forgiving their sin. That's truly Amazing Grace.

It's also important to know that it wasn't just the soldiers who killed Jesus. Because He died for our sins, you can say that each of us had a part in Jesus dying. He died for all sins, including the ones you have done on purpose and the ones done by accident. And now we have a new life with Him!

Jesus forgave those who killed Him, but what about Corrie ten Boom? Was she ever able to forgive that guard? In her book, *The Hiding Place*, Corrie says she forced herself to say the words of forgiveness to this guard—and then a miracle occurred.

As she shook his hand, she says "An incredible thing took place. The current started in my shoulder, raced down my arm, sprang into our joined hands. And then this healing warmth seemed to flood my whole being, bringing tears to my eyes. 'I forgive you, brother!' I cried. 'With all my heart!'"

With God's power, Corrie forgave, and it felt as if she had been freed from prison.

CHALLENGE

Imagine that you had a friend over to play, and the $20 you kept on your dresser went missing after the person left. Here are two different scenarios. Think about how you would feel in each situation.

1. STICKY FINGERS

Your friend admitted she had found a $20 bill stuck to the bottom of her backpack when she got home. She didn't know where it came from, and she had spent it already. You could see she felt really bad about taking your money, but it was an accident.

How would you feel? _____

What would you do? _____

#FORGIVINGCHALLENGEKIDS

2. FINDERS KEEPERS

What if that friend confessed to taking the money even though she knew it was yours? The friend laughed, saying, "Finders Keepers, Losers Weepers!" and would not give it back.

How would you feel? _____

What would you do? _____

Which scenario would hurt you more?

☐ Sticky Fingers   ☐ Finders Keepers

How much did you lose in the Sticky Fingers story? _____

How much did you lose in the Finders Keepers story? _____

Note that you lost the exact same amount in both stories. So why do you think the Finders Keepers story makes you feel worse?

_____

_____

Corrie ten Boom said that the people who learned to forgive their enemies after World War II were able to rebuild their lives. But the people who held on to their anger did not. Why?

_____

_____

_____

_____

THE MESS-UP • 69

DAY 11

THE MESS-UP: SIN
HURTS BY LOVED ONES

HEROES AND VILLAINS

In the TV show, *Scooby Doo*, Shaggy and Scooby are the only two characters who have appeared in every single show, spin-off, episode, or movie. And they are always the heroes. They save the day by preventing the villains from stealing or destroying something good. Everything is usually simple and clear in cartoons. The bad guy is always bad, and the good guy will save the day.

Real life is not always like that. Occasionally, the people who are our heroes hurt us. And sometimes we hurt the people we care about the most, like our best friend or our siblings. People in the Bible had problems with their siblings too.

LOVE MEANS SAYING 'I'M SORRY'

Hurts from someone you trust or love can be the most painful of all.* If you are hurt by someone you love, then you may begin to lose your trust in them. You might feel double the pain because not only are you hurt, but the relationship is broken.

In Genesis, there is a story about a young man named Joseph, one of 12 sons of Jacob. Joseph was shown favoritism by his father, who gave him a special colorful

---

*NOTE TO FACILITATORS: See page 270 at the end of the book for more information on hurts from loved ones.

coat. The other brothers were very jealous of the attention he got, so they plotted their revenge.

One day, the other brothers found Joseph alone in the fields. They grabbed him, took his coat, and hurled him into a well. The original plan was to kill him, but they decided to make some money by selling him as a slave. Then they lied and told their father that Joseph had been killed by wild animals.

So Joseph found himself taken to Egypt, miles from his family. He was a slave, all because of what his brothers did. He could have been very angry and bitter.

But God was with Joseph in Egypt. Even though he found himself unfairly treated and even thrown into prison, God used his bad situations for good. Eventually, by interpreting dreams for the Pharaoh, Joseph was given the very powerful job of second-in-command in Egypt. Talk about a turnaround!

Many years later, Joseph's brothers came to Egypt looking for food. A famine in the area left them desperate and hungry. When they came to the palace, they did not even recognize Joseph, but he knew who they were. Then Joseph ordered that their little brother, Benjamin, be arrested for stealing a precious cup (which he didn't really do). The brothers were terrified. They were certain that they were receiving payback for what they had done to their other brother, Joseph.

One of the brothers, Reuben, said, **"Didn't I tell you, 'Don't hurt the boy'? But no, you wouldn't listen. And now we're paying for his murder." Genesis 42:22 (The Message)**

When we cause deep cuts or are hurt badly, we remember it, even years later. The brothers remembered what they did to Joseph.

Finally, in the big climax, Joseph let Benjamin go free and revealed his true identity to the brothers. **"I am Joseph your brother whom you sold into Egypt. But don't feel badly, don't blame yourselves for selling me. God was behind it. God sent me here ahead of you to save lives." Genesis 45:4 (The Message)**

Can you imagine? Joseph's brothers had tried to kill him and then sold him into slavery. And yet he forgave them because he could see God working, even though his brothers had abandoned him.

HOW DEEP IS THE FATHER'S LOVE

The one person who knows more about deep cuts from loved ones than anyone else is Jesus. When He was on the cross, He called out to God the Father:

"My God, my God, why have you forsaken me?" **Matthew 27:46b**

We know that Jesus had deep cuts on His body because of the nails and thorns. You may not realize this, but the biggest cut Jesus received was on the inside when He was abandoned by God. The one He loved the most, God the Father, had to desert Him so that we could be freed from our sin.

After three days, Jesus rose from the grave, giving us forgiveness and healing the deepest cuts in our lives. This is greater than our wildest dreams.

CHALLENGE

Jesus was nailed to the cross for you and me. Do the following activity to learn how our actions leave scars.

1. Find a scrap piece of wood, a hammer, and a nail. With adult supervision, drive that nail into the wood. When we mess up, sin drives hurt into others, like a nail going into wood.

#FORGIVINGCHALLENGEKIDS

❷ Next, turn the hammer around and pull out the nail. What is left in the wood? Even though we can take out the nail, a scar will remain.

❸ Think or talk about a time a loved one hurt you. This could be a teacher, friend, Dad, Mom, sister, brother, cousin, aunt, grandpa, grandma, uncle, aunt, neighbor, classmate, or coach. Write or draw about the experience in the box below.

❹ Finally, put that piece of wood with the nail hole somewhere to remind you that hurts leave scars, but Jesus came to forgive even the deepest cuts.

RED ALERT!

Jesus's family tree had some very flawed people in it. Solomon married 700 women, David had a man killed to steal his wife, and Rehoboam and Abijah were described as evil and sinful. God doesn't choose perfect people to carry out his Grand Plan.

DAY 12

THE MESS-UP: SIN
HURTS IN THE WORLD

9/11

In New York City, a five-year-old girl named Nicole Foster was getting ready for school. She had a red dress on and couldn't wait for her new kindergarten teacher to see it. As she ate breakfast, she let her legs swing back and forth, imagining how she was going to fly higher than ever on the playground swing.

As she walked with her dad to school, she grabbed his hand and joked, "Don't step on a crack or you'll break your mama's back!" She gave him a squeeze as he dropped her off at school. "See you after work, Dad!" she called after him.

On that day, September 11, 2001, Nicole's dad never came home.

Nicole's dad, Noel J. Foster, worked on the 99th floor of the South Tower of the World Trade Center. At 8:46 a.m., a jet airplane flew dangerously low and headed straight for the North Tower. In a matter of seconds, hijackers flew the plane into the building, and it slammed into floors 93 through 99.

A second plane flew into the South Tower, a third plane flew into the Pentagon building outside of Washington D.C., and a fourth plane crashed in central Pennsylvania.

Everyone on all four planes were killed, including the 19 hijackers. At 10:28 that morning, the twin towers collapsed, killing 2,606 innocent people.

In all, 2,977 people died on September 11.

PICKING UP THE PIECES

Terrorism is a terrible tragedy. Terrorists hurt others to get money or power over them or because they're angry that people look or think differently. None of these reasons are right or fair. But life has always been unfair ever since the Garden of Eden; those who understood this as much as anybody were the people of Israel.

The people of Israel were oppressed by a nation called Babylon. Babylon conquered Jerusalem in 587 B.C. and forced the people to leave their home. The Babylonians used the Israelites as slaves and no longer allowed them to live as a holy nation that God set apart.

The prophet Jeremiah wrote a prayer, pleading with God to rescue them.

> **"God, pick up the pieces.**
>   **Put me back together again.**
>   **You are my praise!**
> **Listen to how they talk about me:**
>   **'So where's this "Word of God"?**
>   **We'd like to see something happen!'**
> **But it wasn't my idea to call for Doomsday.**
>   **I never wanted trouble.**
> **You know what I've said.**
>   **It's all out in the open before you.**
> **Don't add to my troubles.**
>   **Give me some relief!"**
>
> **Jeremiah 17:14-17 (The Message)**

Sometimes we have to forgive people whom we don't even know—like the terrorists of 9/11. We need God's help to forgive people who do evil things in the world. Maybe they didn't hurt us personally, but they hurt our country and the people in it.

God tells us to pray for the injustice in the world. King David did just that; he prayed for his nation when enemies were attacking.

> "I call to you, God, because I'm sure of an answer.
>   So—answer! bend your ear! listen sharp!
> Paint grace-graffiti on the fences;
>   take in your frightened children who
> Are running from the neighborhood bullies
>   straight to you."
> Psalm 17:6-7 (The Message)

Even when terrible things happen, and even when evil people do awful things, we know we can run straight into the arms of Jesus. He is the only one who can pick up the pieces. He is the only one who can put our broken world back together.

CHALLENGE

Write out your own Forgiveness Prayer for the hurts caused in our world using the verses from Jeremiah. Choose an unfair hurt in the world from the list below or use your own idea to write this prayer.

UNFAIR HURTS

- Divorce
- Cancer
- Death
- War
- Famine
- Pandemics
- Hurricanes
- Earthquakes/Floods

#FORGIVINGCHALLENGEKIDS

FORGIVENESS PRAYER:

"God, pick up the pieces.

Put _____ back together again. You are my praise!

See how _____

_____ never wanted trouble.

You know what I've said. It's all out in the open before you.

Give _____ some relief!

Amen."

RED ALERT!

Jeremiah was one of the most famous prophets in the Old Testament. When he prophesied that Babylon would conquer Israel, King Zedekiah tried to kill him by throwing him in a cistern. But he was rescued by a Cushite man. It turned out that Jeremiah was right all along. In 587 B.C., Babylon conquered Jerusalem.

DAYS **13-19**
OF THE 40-DAY CHALLENGE

THE 'FESS-UP:
CONFE

SSION

THE MOUNTAINS OF REDVALE

PART 3

After saying goodbye to Bob the Cave Whale, the group began to work their way up the side of Mount Goel. The path was steep and rocky, but so far it was surprisingly wide. Isabella's leg was still hurting, so Malachi insisted that she ride on Balthazar.

"Sooooo…I guess you messed up big time," Red said to Isabella, suddenly popping up on her left side.

"What do you mean I messed up?" Isabella said. "It was Emily and Aiden who dug the pit and started all of this. I told them not to do it."

"I don't think Red is talking about that," said Balthazar, twisting his head around to look at Isabella. "I think he's talking about what's been happening to you on social media and at school."

Isabella's heart sank. "Oh. That."

"To be honest, I'm happy Redvale doesn't have the internet," Red said. "People in your world seem to use it mainly for being mean to each other."

"The internet is not all bad," Isabella said. "It can be helpful."

"True. But it wasn't very helpful when kids started teasing you on TikTok and Clubhouse," said Balthazar. "They were merciless."

Isabella sighed. It hurt to even think about what had happened. After their first visit to Redvale, kids found out that she believed in another world, and they teased her mercilessly. So, she decided to keep their second trip to Redvale a secret. But just when the teasing was dying out, someone spread stories on social media that she not only returned to Redvale, but she believed animals there could talk. Kids started sending her videos of their pets and asking if she could talk with

#FORGIVINGCHALLENGEKIDS

them. One girl asked if she wanted to chat on Clubhouse with her gerbil. Another started sending text messages from her turtle.

"You thought the culprit was your new friend, didn't you?" Balthazar said. "You thought she gave away your secret."

How do they know so much about what's been happening? But it was true. Isabella had recently made friends with a girl named Nova. One day, when they were hanging out together and having so much fun, Isabella let down her guard. She let slip something about her second trip to Redvale. That's why she thought Nova had to be the one who gave it away.

To get her revenge, Isabella revealed one of Nova's secrets on social media. She told the world that Nova felt bad about the size of her nose. Within hours, kids were calling Nova "Pinocchio."

"Like I said," Red pointed out. "You really messed up, didn't you?"

There was no denying it. What's worse, she later talked to some other friends, and they convinced her that it *wasn't* Nova who revealed the secret about her second trip to Redvale. She still didn't know who the culprit was, but it probably wasn't her new friend.

Now, Nova wasn't talking to her, and she felt horrible about everything. For the past two weeks, she hid from others. She avoided friends in the school hall and stayed away from social media. If she could've crawled into a hole, she would have.

"Getting revenge often has a way of backfiring," Balthazar said. "It hurts you just as much, or even more, than it hurts the other person."

"But Malachi always likes to say that after you mess up, you need to 'fess up!" Red said.

"'Fess up?"

"Confess. Admit your sin," said Balthazar. "That's the second big step on the path to forgiveness."

"And speaking of paths, things are beginning to look a bit tricky here," Red said. He slipped behind Balthazar and Isabella because the path had narrowed.

THE MOUNTAINS OF REDVALE • 81

There was barely room for one donkey. To their right, the cliff plunged straight down, and Isabella hoped that Balthazar was sure-footed. She didn't like the idea of tumbling off the edge and onto the rocks below. It was a long way down.

REACHING THE PEAK

Aiden stayed as far to the left as possible and tried not to look down. It made him dizzy to be so close to the edge.

"What if this volcano erupts when we get to the top?" he asked Malachi, who was hiking just in front of him, carrying his staff.

"That would not be a good thing. Let's pray it doesn't happen."

As if the mountain sensed Aiden's fears, it began to rumble and shake. Aiden gripped the side of the wall to stay on the path and keep from plunging over the cliff.

"This whole mission seems crazy and dangerous," he said when the shaking mercifully stopped.

"Being a peacemaker is dangerous business," Malachi said. "But it's the right path."

"Being a peacemaker?" Aiden asked. "I thought this was a rescue mission!"

"But peacemakers *are* rescuers," Malachi said, "When you make peace with others, you rescue your relationship."

"But we're not friends with Frankie and Chloe. Far from it."

"By being peacemakers, maybe you'll *create* a new friendship."

"Whatever," Aiden muttered under his breath.

At last, they reached the top of Mount Goel, where they got a tremendous view of Redvale from every direction. Looking to the west, they could see the Red Desert stretching to the horizon. And they could see tiny villages scattered among the foothills of the Crimson Mountains. Looking to the east, they could see the deep, green canopy of the forest. There were trees as far as the eye could see—although if Aiden squinted, he could also make out the Scarlet Sea in the far distance.

#FORGIVINGCHALLENGEKIDS

"It's beautiful," said Emily. "If we weren't standing on top of a volcano, I'd suggest we stay here forever."

"No time for that," Aiden said. "We need to get Frankie and Chloe and get out of here. How do we find them?"

Malachi walked to the very edge of the enormous crater leading into the center of the volcano. "We go down," he said.

Aiden shuffled to the edge of the crater. Ever so carefully, he leaned over and peered into the black hole. "I was afraid you were going to say that."

"You have to go down before you can rise," Malachi said. "Jesus went into the tomb before he rose."

"Tomb?" Red exclaimed. "Are you saying this is going to be our tomb? That we're going to die in there?"

"No, I'm simply saying that going down into this volcano is *like* going into a tomb," Malachi said. "It's like dying to ourselves."

"I still don't like the sound of that," Red said. "Anything with the word 'dying' is not a good thing."

"'Dying to ourselves is the Bible's way of saying we must give up our pride," Malachi said. "We must give up our desire to always be right. We must admit that sometimes we're wrong and mess up."

"You're talking about the 'fess-up part, aren't you?" said Aiden.

"That's right. Confessing our sins is like plunging into a deep hole. It's scary."

As Aiden continued to peer into the void, he could hear strange sounds coming from below. And the stink! It smelled like a thousand gym lockers filled with a million stinky socks.

"Follow me," Malachi said. He motioned toward a narrow path that led down, down into the very heart of the volcano. For the longest time, no one moved or said a thing. They just stared back at Malachi.

At last, Balthazar began to clomp toward the path.

"We better get started," he said, disappearing into the dark. The others followed close behind.

THE MOUNTAINS OF REDVALE

BLESSED ARE THE PEACEMAKERS

As they streamed down into the volcano in single file, Emily stared up at the circle of light above her head. The light streaked downward, revealing the path at their feet—but barely. The deeper they went, the darker it got.

"I still don't understand what I have to 'fess up about," Emily grumbled to Malachi.

"If you don't know, then you need to go deeper," he said.

"Isn't that what we're all doing? Going deeper?"

"So we are."

"Tell her about fight and flight, Malachi!" said Red excitedly. He sounded awfully cheerful considering they were in a volcano.

"What's he talking about—fight or flight?" Emily asked. She was looking for something to take her mind off of the smell and gurgling sounds of the volcano.

"When people feel threatened and in danger, they often do one of two things," Malachi said. "They respond with either 'fight' or 'flight.'"

"Flight? What does hopping on an airplane got to do with feeling threatened and in danger?" she said.

Red giggled, which irritated her.

"By 'flight,' I mean that some people run away when they're feeling threatened. They flee," said Malachi. "But other people respond to threats by fighting back."

"I know which one you are," Aiden said to Emily. "You fight. You fight, even when you're *not* threatened."

"I do not!" Emily punched Aiden in the back.

"I wouldn't talk, Aiden!" said Red. "You too fight when you're in danger."

"That's why you and Emily decided to get your revenge on Frankie and Chloe," Malachi said. "It was your way of fighting back."

"What's Isabella's way of responding to trouble?" Red asked.

Emily knew the answer, but Malachi spoke before she could blurt it out. "Let's ask Isabella. What do you think?"

#FORGIVINGCHALLENGEKIDS

Isabella was ahead of Emily on the path, barely visible. She heard Isabella say, ever so softly, "I react by running away."

"That's what I was going to say!" Emily said triumphantly.

"But there's a third way of reacting to troubles besides fight or flight," Malachi said.

He paused and turned to face the kids. "The third way is to be peacemakers. When you fight, you focus on defeating your enemy, and when you react with flight, you focus on saving your skin. But by being a peacemaker, you focus on *both* of you. You try to create peace."

"Easier said than done," Emily said.

"You can say that again," Red said.

"Easier said than done," she repeated.

"And you're exactly right," Malachi added. "Being a peacemaker can be the most difficult path."

As everyone went quiet for a moment, Emily realized that the darkness had become even deeper. She stared up at the top of the volcano, where the circle of light had shrunk. She was about to ask what happens when they can't see the path in front of them when she suddenly heard the flapping of wings in the dark.

"What's that?"

"Duck!" Balthazar shouted.

As Emily ducked, she felt and heard something huge come flapping only inches above her head. Even worse, it didn't sound like the creature was alone.

SHADOW BATS!

Isabella's first desire was to run. But it's not easy running when you're on a perilous path corkscrewing deep into a volcano. So she ducked and covered her head as one of these creatures swooped directly above, only inches away.

In the dark, she couldn't see the creatures; she could only hear them and smell them. She could hear flapping, so they obviously had wings. Crouching, she moved into a ball and hoped the creatures couldn't see her in the dark. Suddenly, she felt a great darkness come over her like a cloak, as if she were being covered in ink. It made her feel incredibly sad and helpless.

"What are these things?" Aiden shouted.

"Shadow bats!" Red exclaimed. "They're shadows that fly and attack!"

Shadow bats. That's exactly how Isabella felt. She felt as if a shadow had come over her. She wanted to fight back, but how do you fight a shadow? Shadows don't have bodies. She felt another one of the creatures land on her and cloak her in shadow, adding another layer of darkness. Then a third creature landed on her back, and she felt a great weight pressing down on her. Layer after layer of shadow.

Emily must've figured out what was happening because she suddenly shouted, "The creatures got Isabella! We gotta do something!"

What could be done? Isabella thought. She was buried in shadows. It was hopeless. She had a made a mess of things at school, and she didn't know if she could ever go back there again. The darkness got heavier and heavier.

Since their last visit to Redvale, Isabella had buried herself in the Bible. She had been memorizing Scripture each and every day. But now, with the shadows weighing down, she had a difficult time working up the energy to recite Scripture.

But she had to try. So she began, stammering. "God is…God is light. He's light and in Him…in Him there is no darkness…no darkness at all!"

She remained in a ball on the ground, with her head down, but she suddenly felt something warm. Even with her face buried in her arms, she could sense a glow.

"It's working!" Aiden shouted.

Whatever was happening, Aiden was right. She felt the darkness begin to lift from her back, as if shadows were being peeled away, one by one, layer by layer. At last, she raised her head, and she could finally see her attackers. They were shadows in the shape of bats, and they were fleeing from the light. But where was this light coming from?

#FORGIVINGCHALLENGEKIDS

Isabella looked over and saw Malachi holding up a light, which was driving away the shadow bats.

"The people living in darkness have seen a great light!" Malachi shouted, as the bats screeched and flew away as fast as they could. "On those living in the land of the shadow of death a light has dawned!"

Isabella knew those words too. She had memorized them. Matthew 4:16. They were spoken by Jesus, but they were also spoken by the prophet Isaiah.

Red held on to Malachi's staff, as their leader used both hands to hold the light high in the air. She couldn't see what he was holding, but he kind of looked like Moses raising the Ten Commandments above his head.

Emily rushed to her side. "Are you all right, Isabella?" Then both Emily and Aiden helped her to her wobbly feet.

"I'm all right now," she said.

"You were covered in shadows," Aiden said. "I thought you were a goner."

The three Perez kids stared down into the volcano. With Malachi's light, they had a good view of the rocky, craggy walls leading down into further darkness. They could also see the shadow bats, hundreds of them, trying to escape the light. The bats fled into the pit.

"What is that light you're holding?" Isabella asked.

With the shadow bats gone, Malachi finally lowered the light. As he did, the light dimmed just a bit—enough for the kids to see that the glow was coming from a book. But not just any book.

"The Big Wilderness Guidebook is also a light," Malachi said. "It has a way of driving away the shadows."

"Why didn't you get out the guidebook sooner?" Emily asked, almost as if she were mad he didn't.

"I did have it out. Didn't you notice?"

Isabella had to admit. In the dark, she didn't see Malachi holding the Big Wilderness Guidebook.

"But not to worry," Malachi said. "It's often the case that people don't see this light until things get the darkest."

With the shadow bats gone and the light leading the way, the group continued their steady descent into the center of the volcano. Every so often, the mountain would rumble and steam would shoot out from the walls. They could also hear a gurgling coming from various holes.

"Is slime making that sound?" Emily asked.

"It is," said Balthazar. "But try not to let the sound bother you. Keep your eyes on the path."

The deeper they went, the darker it got. But the darker it got, the brighter the light in Malachi's hands shone. They began to see writings on the wall in unknown languages. Sometimes they saw pictures of what appeared to be soldiers fighting battles with swords and spears.

Deeper and deeper they went until Isabella wondered if the path would ever end. But then…

Voices. Very faint voices.

"Help!"

"I see a light coming! Do you see the light?" came one of the voices.

The voices were coming from below, but they were very faint.

"Helloooooooo down there!" Red shouted. "Can you hear us!!"

"We hear you! Who are you?" shouted the first voice—a boy's voice. It must be Frankie.

"Hurry!" hollered the second voice—Chloe.

They picked up the pace, but not too much. One wrong step, and they might fall off the path and into the darkness. The gurgling got louder, and the smell got worse. Isabella wished she had one of the masks she had worn during the pandemic to cover her nose.

"I see you!" shouted Frankie. By this time, it was clearly his voice. "I see the light!"

"Hurry, hurry!" Chloe shouted.

#FORGIVINGCHALLENGEKIDS

Why did she keep urging them to hurry? Didn't she know that if they hurried too fast, they might fall?

But as they got closer to the bottom of the mountain, the light revealed why Chloe wanted them to move as fast as they could. The two kids were stuck in goo up to their waists, and more slime was slowly sliding down on them.

This rescue was going to be a lot stickier and trickier than they thought.

TO BE CONTINUED ON PAGE 124.

DAY 13
THE 'FESS-UP: CONFESSION
WHO SAYS WHAT'S BAD OR GOOD?

THE HOT TUB DILEMMA

Emmett and Charlie were excited to get into the hot tub at their hotel. So they raced each other down the hallway, anxious for the warm bubbles and relaxing jets. A safety sign was posted next to the hot tub, and Charlie paused to skim the rules. The third rule made him freeze.

HOT TUB RULES

NO JUMPING OR DIVING

LIMIT YOUR SOAK TIME TO 15 MINUTES

NO CHILDREN UNDER THE AGE OF 12 ALLOWED IN HOT TUB

"Hey Dad, I don't think we can go in." Charlie said. "The sign says no one under 12, and I'm only 11 and Emmett's 9."

"That stinks! The hot tub at our last hotel said 'Under 16 Needs Adult Supervision,'" Emmett said, reading over Charlie's shoulder.

"We've always been allowed to go in the hot tubs!"

Dad came over and studied the sign carefully.

"It looks like this hotel doesn't want kids to use their hot tub." he agreed.

"What a joke." Charlie said, glancing around the room for any sign of cameras or another person. There were none in sight.

"Should we just get in anyway?" he said. "After all, we've been in tons of hot tubs in the past. And I'm almost 12."

"Why doesn't every hotel have the same rules?" Emmett asked. "Who says what's right and what's wrong?"

What do you think they should do?

☐ Pretend they didn't see the sign and go in.

☐ Follow the rules and use the pool instead.

RULES OF LIFE

As Emmett and Charlie discovered, rules are not always fair. Sometimes, the rules are different, depending on where you live, how old you are, or who is in charge. Although the hot tub rules were different at different hotels, at least a sign was there to spell out the rules clearly. But what do we do when there isn't a sign to tell us the rules? It's not always easy to know what's right or wrong in life.

Some people think they set all of the rules for their own life. Maybe you've seen some of these sayings:

These might seem like fun little phrases on a journal or poster, but they really don't make sense. If we actually live our life by these signs, then forgiveness will be even harder because no one would ever be wrong.

- If you make your own rules, then you don't need to confess or apologize to anyone, because according to YOUR rules, you are innocent.

- If you are the boss of your own life, no one can tell you that you're not following the rules or you're not on the right path. Who are they to say?

These popular sayings really don't line up with what we believe as Jesus followers.

THY WORD IS A LAMP

God doesn't make rules to keep us from having fun or selfishly wanting to control us. He is the Creator, and He knows best how things should work. **"Trust in the**

#FORGIVINGCHALLENGEKIDS

Lord with all your heart and lean not on your own understanding; in all your ways submit to him, and he will make your paths straight." Proverbs 3:5-6

It's for our own good that God tells us what is right and wrong. His rules make us feel safe and loved, and they open us up to being even more creative. God's rules are not complicated. He tells us in the Bible how we should live through the Ten Commandments. (You can read about those in Exodus 20:1-17.)

But God didn't stop there. His plan wasn't to just give us rules to follow perfectly, because we can't. No one, except Jesus, is perfect. He offered Himself up as a sacrifice for us so that we are forgiven even when we don't get the rules right.

At the same time, Jesus's forgiveness doesn't mean we can throw out the rules. If we say, "I'm going to sin because I'm going to be forgiven anyway," then are we truly following Jesus? We must still try our best to follow God, knowing we are forgiven when we mess up. It's not up to us to decide who's right or who's wrong. God has done that for us. He announced to the world that we are His good children.

So let's go back to Emmett's question: Who says what's bad and what's good? God does!

Emmett ran past the hot tub and did a cannonball into the pool. Charlie was right behind him, matching splash for splash. A hot soak would have felt good, but it's hard to beat the feel of a perfect cannonball!

While it's not always easy to follow the rules, we can be thankful that God puts those laws into place for our good. It's the best way to make a splash in this world.

CHALLENGE

Write out the Ten Commandments on the stone tablets below. You can find the commandments in Exodus 20:1-17. Remember who is in charge. Remember that the God who makes the rules helps us 'fess up when we mess up.

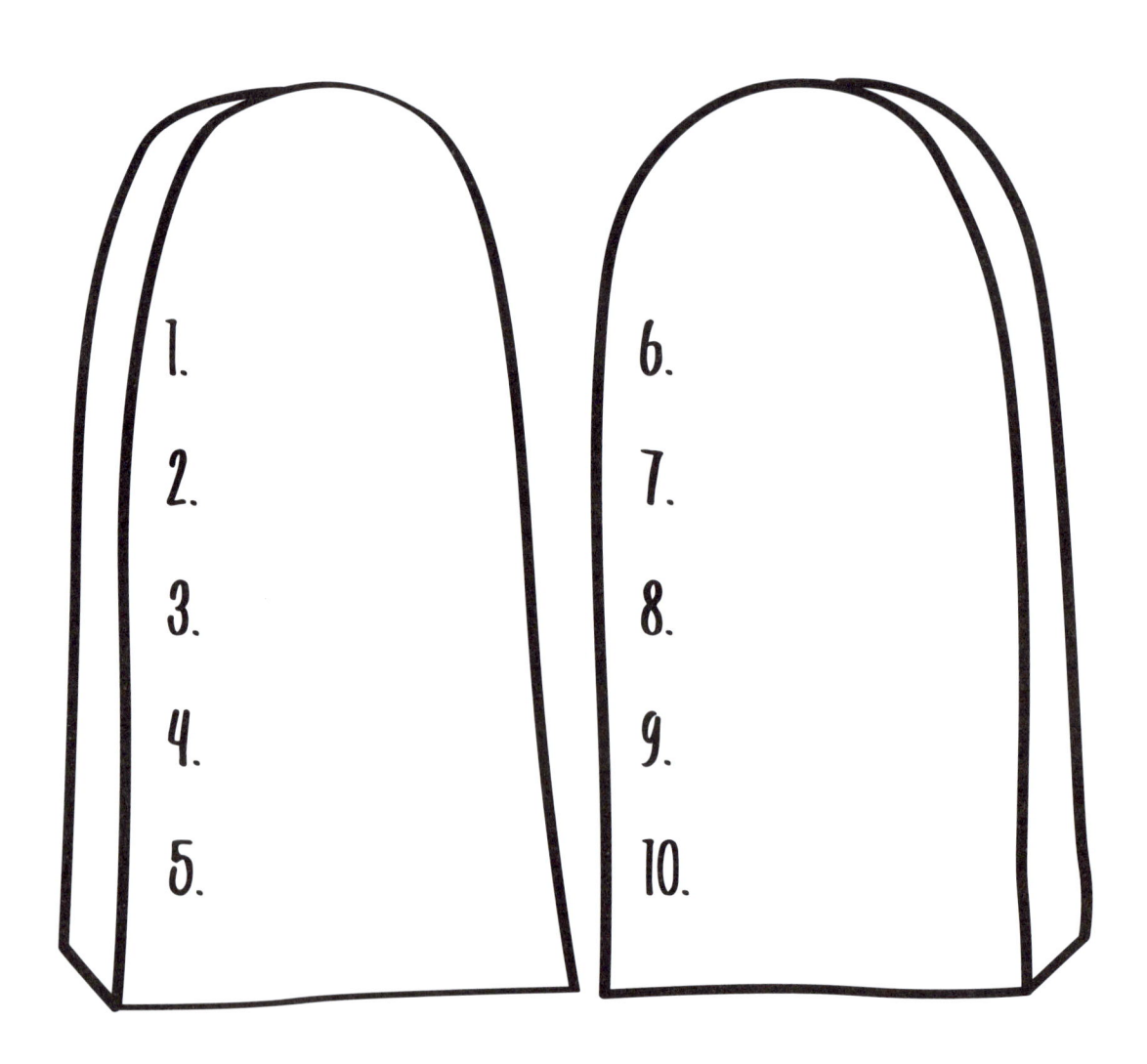

1.
2.
3.
4.
5.

6.
7.
8.
9.
10.

#FORGIVINGCHALLENGEKIDS

RED ALERT!

> Mountains are often thought of as holy places in the Bible. God spoke to Moses in a burning bush at Mount Horeb (Exodus 3). Then Moses was given the Ten Commandments on Mount Sinai (Exodus 20). In the Redvale story, we have the fictional "Mount Goel" because "goel" is a Hebrew word for "redeemer." It also means "avenger."

#FORGIVINGCHALLENGEKIDS

DAY 14
THE 'FESS-UP: CONFESSION
FIGHT, FLIGHT, OR MAKING THINGS RIGHT

RUFFLED FEATHERS

Scientists have discovered that animals have two different reactions when they feel threatened or in danger. They call these reactions FIGHT or FLIGHT. Some animals will attack when they're threatened (FIGHT) and some will flee (FLIGHT).

God even designed some animals' bodies to look their scariest when they are planning to fight:

- The hippopotamus will open its mouth and reveal all its teeth.
- Bearded dragons will puff up their necks.
- Rattlesnakes will shake their tail rattles.

Some animals even have "flight" reactions:

- The possum will play dead.
- The chameleon changes colors to hide with the background.

FIGHT OR FLIGHT

Humans have a similar reaction when we feel hurt or are in an emergency. Our bodies prepare for either a fight or flight reaction.

Some of you may clench your fists and begin thinking of ways to get even. That is a fight reaction. Others will want to get away from the situation as quickly as possible and just try to forget it ever happened. That is a flight reaction. Some may even close their eyes and not be able to move. Or you may let someone else take over, giving up your power. This is a freeze reaction, but it's similar to the flight reaction.

Sometimes, long after an emergency or conflict, your body will continue to feel the same fight or flight responses. How often do you remember feeling anger long after the conflict occurred?

All of us have felt both reactions some time in our lives. However, mark down the one you MOST OFTEN choose in an argument.

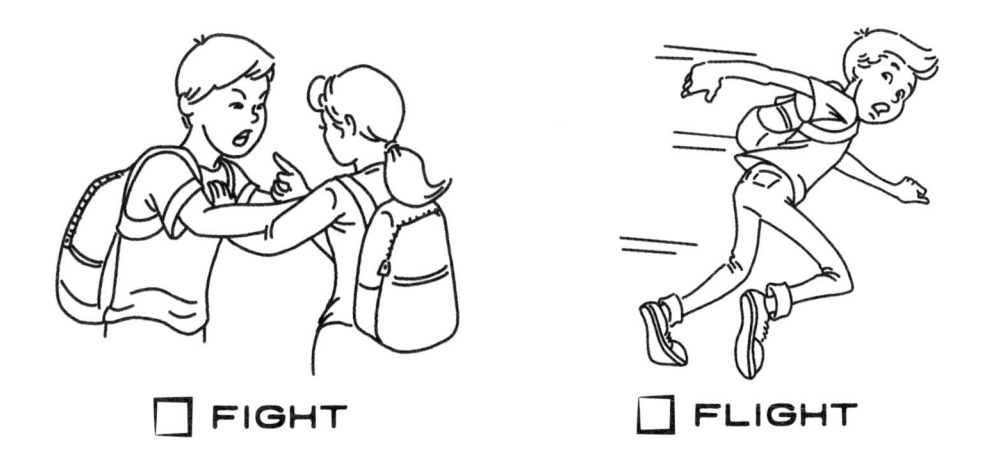

☐ FIGHT   ☐ FLIGHT

Last week, we learned all about the Mess-up—the sin in our world. Sometimes it's not our fault, but other times it is. In both cases, there can be deep hurts on the inside that result from that sin. Those hurts will not go away on their own, no matter how much we fight them or run to get away from them.

So what do we do?

'FESS UP WHEN YOU MESS UP

After we mess up, we 'fess up.

Jesus says that if we go to Him and confess what is on our hearts, He can help us. He knows all about forgiveness, because He took the sin of the whole world on Himself.

Can you imagine what would have happened if Jesus chose fight or flight?

- He could have brought a whole army of angels down and defeated everyone or…
- He could have escaped to the very outer edges of the universe.

Jesus didn't fight and He didn't react with flight. Instead, He offers a third response: **"Blessed are the peacemakers, for they will be called children of God." Matthew 5:9**

Jesus chose the PEACEMAKER response.

When we fight, we're thinking mostly about the other person—how bad they are and how they're going to get what's coming. When we have flight and freeze reactions, we think mostly about ourselves—how we're going to protect ourselves.

Peacemaking is about both. It focuses on the "us." It means we're thinking about our relationship with the other person and how we can fix it. Jesus chose to be a peacemaker, and He went to the cross for our sins. What an amazing Savior we have!

We too can be peacemakers in a 'fight or flight' world.

#FORGIVINGCHALLENGEKIDS

CHALLENGE

Spend some time confessing today. Do you have a safe person to go to, such as a guardian, teacher, parent, or pastor? If you do, write their name below:

_____

Next, write your confession, or 'fess up, below. It may feel scary to confess that you were hurt or that you hurt someone else, but God promises forgiveness. It can feel like a heavy burden is taken off your shoulders!*

THE 'FESS-UP

I'm sorry, I _____

_____

I see that I hurt you by _____

_____

_____

Tell me more about how it made you feel. I want to understand.

Is there something I can do to make _____

_____ right?

I want this to get better.

---

*NOTE TO FACILITATORS: See page 270 at the end of the book for more information on hurts from loved ones.

DAY 15
THE 'FESS-UP: CONFESSION
WHAT'S IN AN APOLOGY?

COSTUME PARTY!
Imagine you were invited to a costume party and you could be whatever you wanted. Draw what costume you would like to wear on the figure below.

SORRY, BUT NOT SORRY

Tara sat in the bathroom stall and tucked up her legs. Tears slipped down her cheeks. She did not want Carmen to know that she was in there and that she was crying.

Tara had not been allowed to go to Carmen's Halloween Party because her parents did not know her family. At school, Tara heard Carmen calling her a "baby" and that she was just a "scaredy cat" for not coming. But that was not true at all! Tara's mom didn't allow her to visit a house where she didn't know the family.

Tara wiped her eyes and swallowed the lump in her throat. It was bad enough to be left out without also being teased for it. Suddenly, a voice echoed through the restroom.

"Tara?"

Tara held her breath. It was Carmen. She knew that Tara had heard her making fun of her and had come to try to make it better. Carmen knocked on the bathroom stall.

"Tara? Come on, I know you're in there. Come talk to me."

"No." Tara sniffed.

"Tara, come on. I didn't mean to hurt your feelings. We were just joking around."

Carmen paused outside the door and put her hand on the handle.

"Tara, it's no big deal. You shouldn't be so sensitive."

After getting no answer, Carmen sighed and turned toward the door.

"You just need to get over it. You're making a fuss over nothing. Well, I tried apologizing, but I guess it didn't work."

Tara came out and went to the sink. As she looked at her reflection in the mirror, she thought, "That wasn't much of an apology. She didn't even say sorry."

THE THREE PARTS OF AN APOLOGY

We are not the best with apologies.

- We don't always realize what we did.
- We often genuinely have a good excuse.
- We have no idea what we could do to make things right.

Carmen thought she was trying to make things better with Tara, but she really wasn't. She was saying all the wrong things.

- She tried to make the hurt she caused look smaller than it was.
- She told Tara how she should feel.
- She made excuses for what she did.

> WE WERE JUST JOKING AROUND.
>
> IT'S NO BIG DEAL.
>
> I DIDN'T MEAN TO HURT YOUR FEELINGS.
>
> YOU'RE MAKING A FUSS OVER NOTHING.
>
> GET OVER IT.

#FORGIVINGCHALLENGEKIDS

An apology is best with three parts to it:

① OWN IT.
Don't make excuses. Own what you did.

② SHOW IT.
Show with your words, expressions, and body language that you are sorry for what happened and that you understand how it hurt the other person.

③ ASK IT.
Ask, "How can I make it right?"

Although it's important to apologize whenever we can, it would be impossible to "own up" to all of the things we ever did in life. We could spend a lifetime apologizing, and it still wouldn't make everything right. That's why we need Jesus. He made all things right. He went to those who were lost, and He tells us to do the same.

Jesus said: **"Go to the lost, confused people right here in the neighborhood. Tell them that the kingdom is here. Bring health to the sick. Raise the dead. Touch the untouchables. Kick out the demons. You have been treated generously, so live generously." Matthew 10:6-8 (The Message)**

Because of His love, we can say, "I'm sorry," and truly mean it.

CHALLENGE

Carmen realized she needed to give a better apology to Tara. Write the apology note from Carmen below using the three parts of an apology. (OWN IT, SHOW IT, ASK IT) If you need help writing, find someone to assist you.

#FORGIVINGCHALLENGEKIDS

RED ALERT!

When Jesus died, the Temple curtain ripped from top to bottom. This massive curtain was 30 feet high, 30 feet wide, and 4 feet thick. It prevented people from entering the Holy of Holies. Because it was torn from the top, it was God's way of showing that He did it. Also, God's was saying that sin could no longer separate us from Him!

#FORGIVINGCHALLENGEKIDS

DAY 16
THE 'FESS-UP: CONFESSION
CONFESSING OUR SIN TO GOD

ME DO IT!

If you have a younger sibling or if you've been around a toddler, you will notice that they go through a phase where they like to do things on their own.

- They like to put on their own shoes: "Me do it!"
- They insist on pouring their own milk: "Me do it!"
- They say they want to walk the dog all by themselves: "Me do it!"

Young kids want to try to do things alone, even if it ends in disaster. As we grow up, sometimes we still have a "Me do it!" attitude. We forget that we have Jesus with us all the time, and we begin to feel as if we have to do everything ourselves.

But God is there to help. He doesn't want you to drown in your misery. He wants to lift you out of the mess, and the way to begin is to confess your sins.

> "Now it's time to change your ways! Turn to face God so he can wipe away your sins, pour out showers of blessing to refresh you, and send you the Messiah he prepared for you, namely, Jesus." **Acts 3:19-20 (The Message)**

But if God knows all of my sins, then why do I need to confess to Him?

God asks us to confess for our own benefit, not His. When God tells you to confess your sins, He knows it will remind you that God is your Savior. He can give you courage to 'fess up when you did wrong.

THE SILENT CONFESSION

Confession to God doesn't always include words. Read the following summary of the Prodigal Son story found in Luke 15:11-32 and see if you can spot the confession.

A man had two sons—an obedient older son and a wild younger son. The wild son couldn't wait to get out of the house, so he asked his father to give him his inheritance. With money in his pocket, the wild son took off for a distant country where he spent everything he had.

When a famine struck the land, the son went hungry. So he took whatever job he could, even feeding pigs—an unclean animal to Jewish people. But he was so hungry that he wished he could eat some of the pig's food.

Finally, the wild son came to his senses. He realized that even his father's servants ate better than him! So he dashed back home. He planned to tell his father that he didn't deserve to be called his son. He was going to beg to be made a servant.

When the father saw him from a long way, he leaped to his feet. The father ran and wrapped his son in a big embrace and kissed him. The son said, "I am not worthy to be called your son." But the father told his servants to give his son the best robe in the house and put a ring on his finger. They were going to cook a fatted calf and celebrate until the cows came home.

The younger son didn't even get a chance to confess to his dad. His dad was so excited that he started the celebration before his son had a chance to say a word.

The father knew that the son's heart had been changed. Without a word, he knew that his son was sorry. It was time to celebrate!

> **"My sacrifice, O God, is a broken spirit; a broken and contrite heart you, God, will not despise." Psalm 51:17**

Our confession to God can be with words, but it doesn't have to be. Sometimes all it takes is that moment when you think to yourself, "Me CAN'T do this." Remember, even if you don't have the words to show your sorrow and regret, God can look even deeper, into your heart. There are not magic words you have to say. Your heart says it all.

> **"Come to me, all you who are weary and burdened, and I will give you rest." Matthew 11:28**

CHALLENGE

Practice a time of silent confession. A great place would be in the safety zone that you identified on Day 2. Set a timer (1 minute is a good start) and find a place with no distractions. Close your eyes and confess your sins. Even if you don't have the right words, know that God is already running to you. You are safe in His arms!

(For more on how the Prodigal Son story ended, check out Day 11 of *Red Letter Challenge Kids* or read about it in Luke 15:11-32.)

#FORGIVINGCHALLENGEKIDS

RED ALERT!

David says in Psalm 32:3-5 that when he refused to confess his sins, his body "wasted away," he groaned all day, and his strength evaporated. This was his B.C. self—Before Confession. After confessing, he says he was fully forgiven and free of guilt. His A.D. self (After Declaration) was free!

#FORGIVINGCHALLENGEKIDS

DAY 17
THE 'FESS-UP: CONFESSION
BE HONEST WITH YOURSELF

A PLANET PROBLEM

Do you remember the names of the planets in our solar system? Color in the Earth below. For more of a challenge, fill in as many names of the planets as you can remember. Then check your answers on page 113.

How did you do? _____ correct answers out of 9.

For much of history, people believed the Earth was the center of the universe. But a devout Christian named Nicholas Copernicus came up with what is called the "heliocentric model." This is the idea that our planets revolve around the sun, not around the Earth.

This idea made quite a stir. Some Christians accepted it, but others didn't, and the disagreements became fierce. Eventually, the final proof that the planets revolved around the sun was discovered in 1838 by a scientist named F.W. Bessel.

PROVE IT!

Often, people don't want to believe something unless it can be proven. It's the same with our laws. People who are accused of a crime in the United States are considered innocent unless proven guilty. In other words, their guilt must be proven or they go free.

"Innocent unless proven guilty" is a vitally important idea in our courts, but it's not the best way to deal with conflicts in our lives. When we know we've hurt someone, it's not helpful to say, "Prove it!"

Nevertheless, some people react to conflicts by saying, "Unless you can prove I hurt you, I'm innocent. I don't have to apologize." But the Bible says that we need to admit to the pain we caused, even if no one can prove it. Even if we think it's not that big a deal.

As 1 John 1:8 says, **"If we claim to be without sin, we deceive ourselves and the truth is not in us."**

Before we can confess to others, we need to get real with ourselves. We need to be honest about the pain we cause and the hurts we feel. Think about other people, not just yourself. The world doesn't revolve around us.

SIN IN THE BALANCE

Sometimes, people refuse to confess the pain they caused because they say the other person caused *more* pain. "Why should I say I'm sorry? You hurt me more than I hurt you!" Or we look for excuses. We say, "Well, I'm not as bad as *that* person" or "At least I didn't do *that*."

It does no good to argue about who hurt the other person more. It's not like you can measure the pain you caused. Leave the fairness up to God. As it says in Proverbs 16:11, **"Honest scales and balances belong to the Lord; all the weights in the bag are of his making."**

Huh? What's that all about?

When selling products in Bible days, stuff was weighed by scales. If you wanted to buy five pounds of spices, for example, a dishonest seller could rig his scales to give you only four pounds. When Proverbs says that "honest scales and balances" belong to the Lord, that means fairness is God's job. Unfairness is not an excuse to avoid confessing.

Thankfully, the Bible doesn't just show us our sin; it also shows us our Savior. Jesus had every excuse in the world to avoid going to the cross. He was innocent, and even when He was taken to court, He was found innocent. It wasn't fair that He was killed, but He accepted the punishment for our sins. He balanced the scales of justice.

CHALLENGE

A great tool for helping you deal with hurts is to make "pardons" in your mind for the other person, rather than immediately blaming them. When someone budges in front of you in line, take a moment to wonder why they did that. Maybe they didn't see you, maybe they really needed to talk to the person ahead of you, or maybe they were in a great hurry.

Practice giving grace and forgiveness below:

SCENARIO 1:

Your best friend seems to like talking to other people more than to you. He picks a different partner in science class.

Possible reason: _____

SCENARIO 2:

The PE teacher always picks you out to do things. It feels like she expects more out of you than others. She calls you out to be the example when doing something new.

Possible reason: _____

SCENARIO 3:

Your neighbor yells at you for throwing your football in the front yard. He even went over and asked your mom if you could only play ball in the backyard.

Possible reason: _____

SCENARIO 4:

Your dad seems to expect perfection from you. You have to get good grades, always be polite and respectful, help out around the house, and give your best in your sports or extracurricular activities. Sometimes it's exhausting.

Possible reason: _____

Answer Key
Planets listed from left to right—Mercury, Venus, Earth, Mars, Jupiter, Saturn, Uranus, Neptune, Pluto

DAY 18
THE 'FESS-UP: CONFESSION
SHADOW CONFESSIONS

SHADOW PUPPETS
Grab a flashlight and find a dark room. Make your own shadow puppets on the wall, using the examples below. Note that with a shadow, all you can see is the outline of the shape. There are no facial features on shadows.

FOX

WOLF

BULL

RABBIT

ELEPHANT

CONFUSION AND CONFESSIONS

Today, we are going to talk about "shadow confessions." What this means is that sometimes we're confused about confessing. For instance...

- What if you don't know if you even did something you need to confess?
- What if you don't know who you might have hurt, if anybody?
- What if you don't know the person who hurt you?

In situations like these, we're in the dark. The other person is like a shadow to us—faceless and featureless. So how can we make "shadow confessions" about "shadow people" whom we don't even know?

Abby faced a problem like this in the story that follows.

FINDERS KEEPERS?

Abby didn't want to walk into her closet. If she did, she knew she would see the blanket on the floor covering the headphones. These weren't just any headphones. They were BuzzEars, the kind that everyone wanted. She had eyed them every time she went shopping, but her mom said they were too expensive.

"Besides," Mom reminded her, "you already have a pair of regular headphones that work fine."

Then something amazing happened. Abby found a brand-new set of BuzzEars left under a tree at the park, partially covered with leaves. No one was around to claim them. *Maybe they've been there a while,* Abby thought. *They're probably broken.*

THE 'FESS-UP • 115

So Abby picked them up and quickly slipped them in the pocket of her jacket. Her mom never noticed, and she never told her.

As soon as she got home, Abby raced upstairs to plug them into her device. To her amazement, the sound came through crystal clear! She looked at herself in the mirror with the BuzzEars on. She had never looked so cool.

But even in her enthusiasm, a pit began to grow in her stomach. What would her mom say when she saw them? She knew that Abby didn't have enough money for them. How could she keep this a secret from her parents?

Finally, Abby decided she had to 'fess up. She got the BuzzEars from under the blanket, where she had hidden them, and headed downstairs. Abby found her mom in the living room, and she explained what had happened.

Then Abby said, "I know I can't keep them, but should I just put the headphones back where I found them? What if they get rained on and ruined? How can I confess to someone I don't even know?"

What do you think Abby should do? Draw or write about it below.

#FORGIVINGCHALLENGEKIDS

BRIGHT AS LIGHT

Like Abby, sometimes we need to confess, even though we're in the dark. We don't know who to confess to, or we're hurt by someone we don't even know. But that shouldn't stop us from confessing our sin.

When you're in the dark, you need a light—and Jesus is that light. What's more, you can become a child of light. As it says in Ephesians 5:8-10, **"For you were once darkness, but now you are light in the Lord. Live as children of light (for the fruit of the light consists in all goodness, righteousness and truth) and find out what pleases the Lord."**

If you're confused about something that you might need to confess or forgive, go to a parent or guardian—and go to God as well.

CHALLENGE

Do you have a shadow confession to make or a shadow person you need to forgive? Write or draw about it in the box below. Recite 1 John 1:8, and pray for those who have "shadows" they need to forgive.

DAY 19
THE 'FESS-UP: CONFESSION
WHAT IF WE'RE INNOCENT?

A HORRIBLE MISTAKE

Anthony Ray Hinton was convicted of a murder he never committed and was put on Death Row. That meant he had to stay in prison until the day he was put to death.

Anthony sat in silence and misery. He hated his life and was angry. But after three years, he accepted that this was going to be his life. He decided that as long as he was on Death Row, he was going to find a new way to live. He chose to bring happiness to others, remembering that God loves and forgives him. Anthony not only changed his own life, but he improved the lives of 54 other inmates around him who were also on Death Row.

According to Anthony's book, *The Sun Does Shine: How I Found Life and Freedom on Death Row*, he faced the jury during his trial and told them, "Jesus was prosecuted, accused falsely for things he didn't do, and all he did was try to love and save this world, and he died and suffered. If I have to die for something I didn't do, so be it. My life is not in the judge's hands. My life is not in your hands, but it's in God's hands."

Twenty-eight years later, in 2015, Anthony was found innocent.

Anthony could have been very bitter when he got out of prison. After all, he spent 28 years in jail for something he never did! Instead, he forgave the people who falsely accused him. Incredible! He could only forgive because he knew Jesus had forgiven him.

Jesus set him free long before the courts did.

HOPE IN A HOPELESS PLACE

When Jesus was arrested, He was taken before a man named Pontius Pilate. Although Pilate did not think that Jesus did anything wrong, the people were stirred up by anger. They shouted, **"Crucify Him!" Matthew 27:11-26**

Dying on a cross was an extreme punishment used for only the worst of criminals. Even if Jesus was guilty, the normal punishment for his crime would have been a stoning. That was less tortuous than crucifixion. Jesus's punishment was completely unfair.

Understanding the unfair treatment of Jesus helped Anthony Ray Hinton to forgive those who accused him falsely and punished him unfairly.

All of us will have times when we're treated unfairly. Maybe you will be accused of something you didn't even do. Or maybe you will be angry at someone who refuses to confess. Note that Anthony didn't wait until he was pardoned before he forgave. He forgave knowing he may be stuck on Death Row for the rest of his life.

Sin can make us feel like we too are on Death Row, because no one can escape death. But even though it can seem hopeless, we don't have to be scared of death. God promises that the blood of Jesus washes us clean of our sin.

God promises resurrection to those who love Him. He brings hope to the most hopeless people and to the most hopeless places. He can turn Death Row into Life Row.

CHALLENGE

It's tough to be accused unfairly. Think about a time you were innocent of something, but you were still blamed for it. Describe or draw about it below. Pray and thank Jesus for taking our sin—for taking our punishment, even though He was innocent.

A TIME I WAS ACCUSED BUT WAS INNOCENT

RED ALERT!

Pontius Pilate gave the people a choice. He could free a murderer named Barabbas. Or he could free Jesus. The people demanded that Barabbas be freed. So Jesus was killed, even though he was innocent. Barabbas the murderer was let go, even though he was guilty. Ironically, some writings say Barabbas's full name was Jesus Barabbas.

#FORGIVINGCHALLENGEKIDS

DAYS 20-26
OF THE 40-DAY CHALLENGE

THE CLEAN-UP:

ABSOL

UTION

HAVE FUN COLORING THIS PAGE!
FIND MORE LIKE THIS AT FORGIVINGCHALLENGE.COM/KIDS

THE MOUNTAINS OF REDVALE

PART 4

Frankie and Chloe stared up from the bottom of the volcano. Slime came up to their waists and held them captive. When they saw Emily and Aiden looking back down from a high ledge, they couldn't have appeared more shocked.

"Emily?" Chloe sputtered.

"Aiden?" Frankie exclaimed.

"What in the world are you doing here?" Chloe asked.

"We're here to rescue you," Emily said. But just saying those words boiled her blood. She lashed out. "You always told us we had to 'pay to pass.' So maybe you need to give us something to be rescued—maybe some Pokémon cards. 'Pay to be saved!' That's our slogan!"

Aiden laughed. "Pay to be saved! I love it, Emily!"

Even Red giggled a little bit.

"Emily!" Isabella shouted. "We've come to pull them out of the slime—not to taunt them!"

"Why shouldn't we taunt them?" Emily said. "They've spent the past year picking on us!"

As Emily spit out those words, the mountain began to shake, and more slime streamed out of a nearby tunnel. The slime flowed into the pit where Frankie and Chloe were trapped, rising to chest level.

"We're sorry, we're sorry!" Chloe yelled.

"Just get us out of here, and we'll never pick on you again!" Frankie shouted.

Hearing their pleas made Emily feel good—good and powerful. Frankie and Chloe were at their mercy. Just the way she liked it.

"You have heard that it was said, 'Love your neighbor and hate your enemy,'" Balthazar said. The donkey came up from behind Emily and peered over her shoulder. **"But I tell you, love your enemies and pray for those who persecute you, that you may be children of your Father in heaven."**

"Jesus said it's easy to love our friends," Malachi pointed out. "The real test is whether we can love our enemies."

How can I argue with Jesus? Emily thought.

"Yes, yes, love your enemies!" Chloe shouted. "Love us!"

Emily turned to Malachi and shrugged. "All right, all right, we'll rescue them. But how?"

"With rope and shovels, of course!" said Red, who began busily rummaging through the saddle packs carried by Balthazar. He tossed down two small shovels and two coils of rope.

"That's it? Just two shovels?" Aiden gasped. "Do you have any others in there?"

Red dove deeper into the bag and dug around. He tossed out a few apple cores and a rubber ducky, which came flying out of the pack. "I always wondered where my rubber ducky went to." Then he popped out his head and gave a shrug. "Sorry. Only two shovels."

"Then who gets the honor of doing the digging?" Emily asked.

Balthazar turned to stare at her. So did Red. So did Malachi. So did Isabella.

"Do you really have to ask?" Red said. "You and Aiden are the ones who need to clean up the mess you made."

"The shovels are yours," Malachi said, offering them the tools. Emily stared at the shovels and sighed. Then she grabbed one of the shovels with a grunt of frustration.

"We don't care who does the shoveling!" Frankie hollered from below. "Just get us outta here!"

"All right, all right," Aiden said. "Be patient!"

#FORGIVINGCHALLENGEKIDS

Malachi attached special belts around the waists of Emily and Aiden. Then, after he hooked the ropes to the belts and to Balthazar's saddle, he began to lower them down from the ledge. Emily and Aiden hung in mid-air, Superman style, with their arms in front and their legs sticking out straight in back. From up above, Isabella used the Big Wilderness Guidebook to shine a light on them as they went deeper and deeper, down to the very bottom of the volcano.

Soon, they were hovering just a foot above the slime, which held Frankie and Chloe in its sticky grip.

"What now?" Emily asked.

"Start digging!" Malachi shouted down to them.

"He wants us to start digging from this position?" Emily said.

"Duh! How else are you going to do it?" Chloe said.

Chloe loved to say, "Duh!" *You'd think she'd be a little more polite to us since we're trying to rescue them,* Emily thought.

Frankie must've thought the same thing because he smacked his sister in the shoulder. "Apologize for saying 'duh.'"

"What? Did I say 'duh'?"

"You know you did," said Aiden.

"It's such a habit that I didn't even know I was doing it. Sorry."

Emily was stunned. Chloe actually said "sorry" about something! That was a small victory. So Emily reached down with her shovel and stuck it into the slime. As the shovel cut into the gunk, it released a puff of something smelly. But at least she was able to scoop the slime relatively easily. She tossed her shovel-load of slime to the side, as far away as possible. Aiden did the same.

"Hey, this isn't as hard as I thought it would be," said Aiden, as he scooped out a second shovel-load of slime. "I think we'll dig you guys out in no time."

"Thank you. We owe you," said Frankie. He actually sounded like he meant it.

"Don't mention it," said Emily in a much kinder tone. But she should've realized that things were too easy to be true. As Emily continued to scoop slime, she spotted movement in a nearby cave. Then she saw several hairy legs appear in the cave doorway. Eight very large legs to be exact.

A huge spider emerged from the cave. A spider the size of a motorcycle!

MIND SPIDERS!

"Be as quiet as you can," Aiden whispered. "Maybe it'll leave us alone."

He tried to scoop the slime silently, but that was easier said than done. As Aiden lifted another shovel-load of slime, he noticed that the huge spider was now standing on a nearby ledge. The spider had eight eyes, and Aiden felt as if all eight of them were looking at him.

Suddenly, the spider shot out a web, and it struck Aiden in the shoulder, sticking to his shirt. Aiden tried to peel it off, but the web stuck like cement.

"Help!"

Aiden was certain that the spider was going to use the web to yank him into its clutches. But that's not what happened. Instead, it seemed as if electricity began traveling down the web. When the electrical current struck Aiden, memories suddenly popped into his mind. It was as if somebody had flicked on a television playing inside his head.

What he saw was a memory—a memory of something that had happened between him and Frankie on the soccer field.

● ● ●

Aiden was having a great game, racing across the deep-green grass with tireless energy. He had already scored two goals, but their team was still behind 3 to 2 with less than a minute to go.

He passed the ball to his team's striker and took off running down the right side of the field. But as he did, Frankie came sprinting alongside him. Frankie was a defender on the other team, and he was a dirty player. They called him The Enforcer for a reason.

#FORGIVINGCHALLENGEKIDS

Just as Aiden was making a move for the goal, Frankie's elbow came out of nowhere and slammed him in the mouth. Then Frankie tripped him up, and Aiden fell flat on his face.

He hit the ground hard, twisting his ankle and tasting turf. He expected to hear the referee's whistle. Maybe Frankie would get a yellow card. Or maybe even a red card and get thrown out of the game.

But no whistle. Frankie had a way of knowing when the referees were looking—and when they weren't. That's how he constantly got away with cheap shots. Some of the fans had noticed, however, and were screaming in protest. But it was no use. Time ran out, and they lost by a point.

When the two teams lined up to shake hands, Frankie nearly broke his fingers when they shook.

• • •

This memory was so clear and real in Aiden's mind, it was as if he were watching it on a TV screen in high def. And it made him furious.

"I remember what you did to me on the soccer field last season!" Aiden suddenly shouted.

"What are you talking about?" Frankie said.

"You gave me an elbow to the mouth and tripped me in the final minute of our game!"

"I don't remember it, but I'm sorry if I did something like that!" Frankie said. "But why are you bringing that up now? You've got to rescue us before the spider gets us all!"

The spider shot out another web, and this one smacked Emily in the back. Once again, the web lit up and electricity zipped along the thick line. Then Emily burst out in anger.

"Chloe, I just remembered what you did to me at school a few weeks ago! You put super-hot sauce on my hot dog in the cafeteria when I wasn't looking. And I nearly went crazy, grabbing people's drinks and chugging them down!"

Strangely, Chloe smiled. "That was pretty funny, wasn't it? I put the 'hot' in hot dog."

Frankie slugged her in the shoulder again. "Chloe, apologize right now!"

"Okay, okay, I'm sorry if you don't like super-hot sauce. But what I'd like to know is why you're thinking about it right now."

The spider shot two more webs, this time striking Aiden and Emily at the exact same moment. Once again, a memory popped into Aiden's mind—another memory of something terrible that Frankie had done to him. It made him so mad that he could spit nails.

"I think I know what's happening," he said, after the memory had flashed before his eyes. "Somehow, this spider is sending memories through her webs—terrible, angry memories."

"Huh?" said Frankie. "Are you sure?"

When the spider shot out two more webs, this time they struck both Frankie and Chloe. Instantly, Frankie's face turn into a vicious scowl.

"What are you remembering?" Aiden asked.

"I'm remembering the two kids who used to go to our school and picked on me and Chloe!" he snarled. "If I could get my hands on them…"

Aiden was stunned. Frankie and Chloe were picked on too? But how could that be? They're the bullies! They're the villains of this story!

"Yeah, and I'm getting a memory of what those kids did to us too!" Chloe said. "The girl named Amy broke into my locker and filled it with chocolate sauce. If I ever see her again, I'll punch her lights out!"

SWOOSH! SWOOSH! SWOOSH!

Like a gunslinger, the spider began firing webs, one after another. Some hit Aiden, some hit Emily, while others struck Frankie and Chloe. Each web shot a memory directly into their minds until all four of the kids were boiling over with anger.

"Cut the webs!" Malachi shouted from above. "Cut the webs!"

But Aiden was too angry to think straight. He heard Malachi tell them to cut

#FORGIVINGCHALLENGEKIDS

the webs, but he was frozen with fury. Besides, they didn't have anything to cut a thick spider web. He soaked up the feelings of anger.

"Use your swords!" shouted Balthazar.

Swords? But they didn't have swords! Aiden was so irritated that he was tempted to shout, "Duh!" at Balthazar.

Before he could say another word, he looked down at the shovel in his hands. Somehow, some way, the golden shovel had been transformed, and it had become a brilliant blade. A golden sword.

"Emily! Look!"

Emily seemed just as startled to see herself holding a golden sword.

"Cut the webs!" Malachi shouted down to them.

They say that spider silk is five times stronger than steel. The only reason we can brush them aside so easily is because spider silk is so thin. But this was a thick web, like rope. It'll be impossible to cut. Or so Aiden thought.

When he took a swing, he was shocked that the sword cut through the web like a knife through peanut butter, sending out sparks. Emily also began slicing away the webs, and more sparks flew into the air. In anger, the spider shot out webs in rapid succession, but Aiden and Emily were too quick. They sliced web after web, faster than the spider could shoot them. It was a mad frenzy of slicing and dicing.

"You're doing great!" Frankie shouted. It seemed so odd to hear encouraging words coming out of his mouth.

Pretty soon, Aiden and Emily had cut away all of the webs, so the spider began firing them even faster. But Aiden and Emily met the challenge, reacting with superhuman speed. Aiden couldn't believe his reflexes were so quick. Sparks filled the air as the webs were hacked apart. But best of all, angry memories no longer filled their minds.

Finally, the spider saw that it was a losing cause, or maybe it ran out of webs. Whatever the reason, it let out a growl of frustration, turned, and disappeared into the darkness of its cave.

"You did it!" Frankie exclaimed, reaching up to give Aiden a high five.

Soaked with sweat, Aiden beamed with pleasure as he returned the high five. Emily did the same with Chloe.

"So how do we dig, now that our shovels have become swords?" Aiden asked. But he didn't need to ask. When he looked down at his weapon, his eyes answered his question. Their swords had transformed back to shovels.

Once again, Aiden and Emily began digging into the slime, deeper and deeper.

"I think I might be able to free myself," Frankie said. He strained to lift his right foot, but the sticky slime wouldn't let go. As Frankie kept at it, the slime suddenly snapped with a POP. Chloe did the same, eventually freeing herself.

Then Aiden reached out his hands and Frankie took hold, like one trapeze artist grabbing hold of another. Emily did the same with Chloe, and then Balthazar began pulling them back up.

When they reached the top, Frankie said, "Thanks," and held out a hand for Aiden to shake. For a moment, Aiden remembered the last time they had shaken hands. It was at the end of the soccer game, and Frankie had squeezed the life out of his fingers. But something new was in the air. Aiden didn't need a Spidey Sense to feel it. So, after a moment of hesitation, he extended his hand, and the two shook. They were enemies no more.

WEBCAMS IN OUR MIND

Emily felt like she was waking up from a dream as she and Chloe also shook hands. Then, even more incredible, Chloe gave her a hug. *Chloe!*

Emily sat down on a rock to catch her breath.

"What in the world just happened?" she said to Malachi. "That spider kept sending memories into our minds. Real memories!"

"You came face to face with a Mind Spider ," Malachi said. "But you conquered it."

#FORGIVINGCHALLENGEKIDS

"Mind Spider? That sounds even creepier than regular spiders," Chloe said.

"They are," said Red. "They send memories into your mind using their webcams."

Aiden laughed. "Spiders don't have webcams!"

"Not the kind of webcams you're thinking of," said Balthazar. "Their webs act like webcams, sending painful memories into our minds. It's their way of immobilizing their victims."

"Victims?" Emily said. "What was it going to do to us?"

"You don't want to know," said Red.

"But I do," said Frankie.

"Regular spiders wrap their victims in webs before they devour them," Malachi said. "Mind Spiders wrap their victims in painful memories."

"Good thing we had these swords—or shovels—or whatever they are," Aiden said, looking at the golden shovel in his hands.

"Whenever you think about those swords, think about forgiveness," Malachi said. "Forgiveness cuts through the bad memories like a sword. It cuts through the tangled webs in our mind."

Everyone went silent as they took in those words. Finally, Chloe just said, "Cool."

"Cool is right," added Frankie.

Then Chloe turned to Emily and said, "I am so sorry, Emily, for everything that I've ever done to you. I'd understand if you never wanted to forgive me."

Emily stared at her and saw a different person. She never knew that Chloe had been bullied as well. That explained a lot.

"Forgive you?" Emily said. "But I've already forgiven you! I did that when I cut those spider webs."

Once again, Chloe and Emily hugged each other.

"And I'm sorry for trying to slime you guys," Aiden said. "It's our fault you ended up in this volcano."

"I'm sorry too," said Emily.

THE MOUNTAINS OF REDVALE • 133

Frankie and Chloe accepted their apologies, and then Chloe turned to Malachi. "Speaking of volcanoes, where are we anyway? One second we were falling into a pit in Verne Park. The next second, we were sliding into a volcano."

"Something tells me that we're not in Florida any longer," Frankie said.

"You're not," said Red, smiling broadly. "Welcome to Redvale!"

Chloe laughed. "A talking fox and a talking donkey! I love it! So the stories that kids at school are saying about Isabella are true. She does talk to animals!"

Isabella blushed.

"We'll set them all straight when we get back to school," Frankie said. "When we're done with them, they'll wish they never teased you, Isabella." He punched his hand as he said these words.

But when Frankie caught the look in Malachi's eyes, he changed his tune. "What I mean to say is that we'll tell the kids the truth about Redvale. I won't punch anyone if that's what you're thinking."

"Although I'd really like to," added Chloe.

Malachi clapped his hands. "All right everyone! We've completed the CLEAN-UP, where you clean up the messes and the anger and the bitterness. But we still have a long way to go."

"Next is the RISE-UP," said Red, looking up. "It's a long, hard climb."

At those words, the mountain began to shake. Rocks broke off from the wall, and a boulder nearly knocked Red in the head. He skipped out of the way just in time. Then steam shot out from holes in the walls all around them, and they heard the gurgling slime from below.

"No time to lose," said Balthazar. "Let's climb!"

TO BE CONTINUED ON PAGE 168.

#FORGIVINGCHALLENGEKIDS

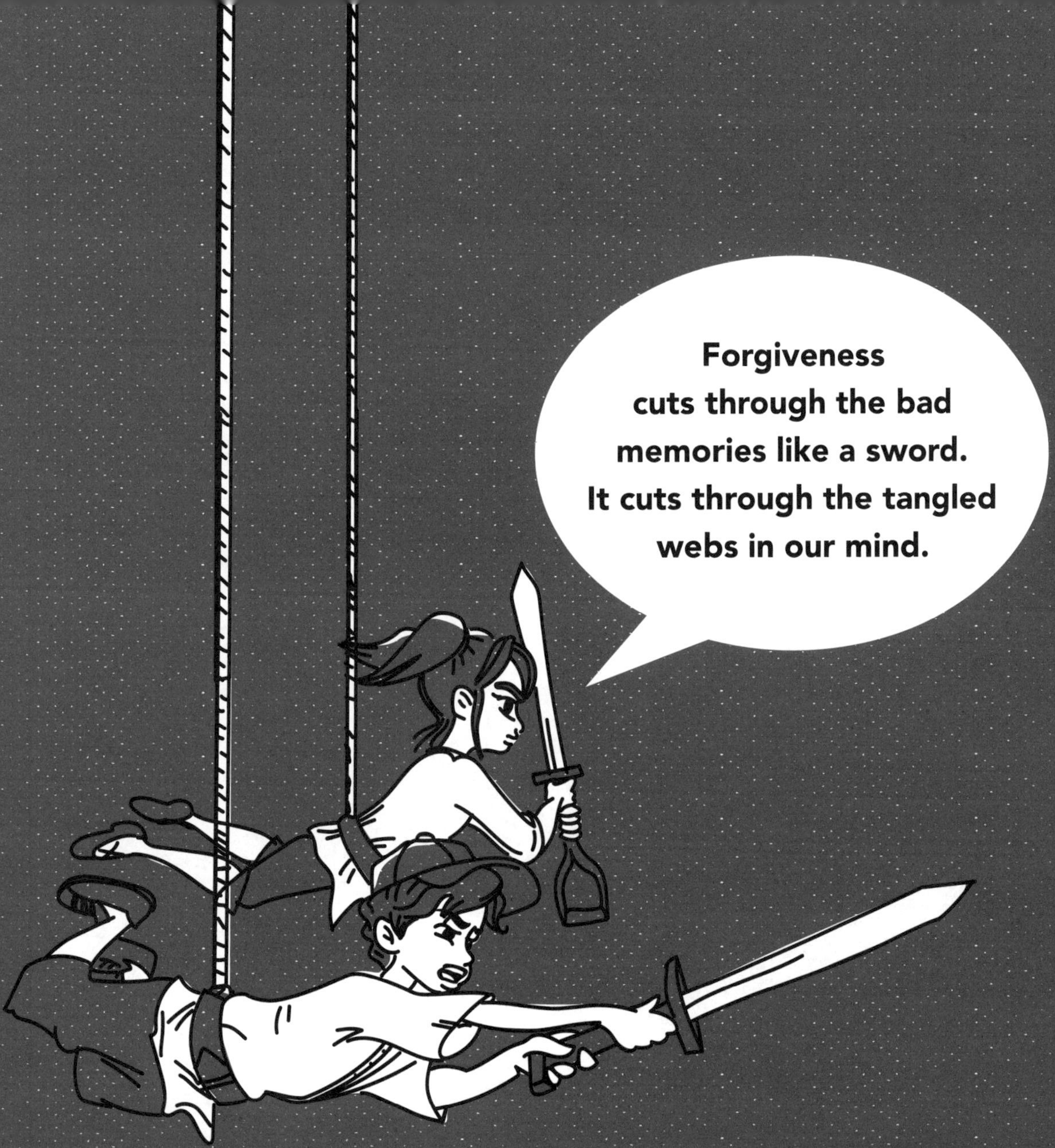

#FORGIVINGCHALLENGEKIDS

DAY 20
THE CLEAN-UP: ABSOLUTION
WHO DO WE FORGIVE AND WHO FORGIVES US?

WHAT IN THE WORLD IS 'ABSOLUTION'?

So far, you've learned about the first two phases of forgiveness:

- The Mess-up (Sin)
- The 'Fess-up (Confession)

Now we are working on the third phase:

- The Clean-up (Absolution)

But what do we mean by "absolution"? This is when God DECLARES that we are "absolved," or forgiven, for the sins we confessed. Our sins are being washed away. That's why we're calling this stage the Clean-up.

THINGS THAT DON'T NEED OUR FORGIVENESS

When we're cleaning up a messy room, we need to know where to put things back. In the same way, when we forgive mistakes, like sorting our hurts, we also need to sort out who needs forgiveness. What gets cleaned up and what doesn't?

Not every hurt or bad feeling needs to be forgiven. The following are three different times where forgiveness wasn't needed.

NATURE

Some African tribes have an interesting practice. When a boy stubs his toe, a friend or parent will hit the rock that he tripped on. Or if a child falls out of a tree, then a brother will go and hit the tree. They are trying to make everything right by striking back at the tree or rock. But that doesn't do a thing to the tree or rock. It doesn't make anything right. Sticks and stones may break our bones, but they don't need our forgiveness. You can't forgive nature.

LOSING GAMES

In 2018, the #1 ranked basketball team in the country going into the NCAA tournament was Virginia. They had lost only two games the entire year. Being the #1 team, they got to play the lowest ranked team in their tournament bracket—University of Maryland, Baltimore County (UMBC). Out of the 16 teams in their bracket, UMBC was ranked 16.

A number one team had never lost in the first round to a #16 seed. Until 2018. Virginia didn't just lose; they lost big—74 to 54! Did Virginia have to forgive UMBC? No. They just got outplayed. We don't have to forgive someone who beats us in competitions.

SINS NOT DONE TO US

Brecken was really upset. It felt as if Tanya, his babysitter, always chose the side of his sister Maren when they were trying to pick games to play. Just because Maren was younger, the sitter always seemed to side with her. It was two against one, and Brecken always lost. So Brecken talked to his mom about it.

Brecken's mom might feel bad or angry about what the sitter was doing. She could even talk to the sitter about the problem. But the mom can't forgive her. Only Brecken could forgive Tanya because he was the one being treated unfairly. We can't forgive others for sins not done to us.

GO TO THE ROCK

Although some hurts and disappointments don't need forgiveness, all pain and suffering in the world comes from sin. Jesus can forgive all sins because all of them are ultimately rebellions against God. When we mess up, we are not only hurting others. We are sinning against God.

Also, even though not all hurts and pain need to be forgiven, you can still take your troubles to Jesus. He cares about you and wants to hear from you. So, if you lose a big game, take your pain to God. He promises to comfort you, even in those situations that don't call for forgiveness.

If you break an arm tripping over a rock, there's no need to kick the rock. (You'll only stub your toe if you do.) Instead, go to the Rock of our salvation. Go to Jesus.

> **"For it is by grace you have been saved, through faith—and this is not from yourselves, it is the gift of God—not by works, so that no one can boast. For we are God's handiwork, created in Christ Jesus to do good works, which God prepared in advance for us to do." Ephesians 2:8–10**

#FORGIVINGCHALLENGEKIDS

CHALLENGE

Today you learned that not all situations need forgiveness. What would you say to the following people who are upset?

1 Your little sister gets furious on family strolls when the dog walks in front of her. She wants to be the line leader.

   Your response: _____

2 Cindy always beats John at checkers, no matter how hard he tries. John gets frustrated at Cindy.

   Your response: _____

3 Your two best friends are in a fight and won't speak to each other. Your coach suggests that you try to make things right.

   Your response: _____

RED ALERT!

When Jesus died on the cross, He said, "It is finished." In the Gospel of John, the Greek word for "It is finished" is *tetelestai*. When a bill was paid in New Testament times, the word *"telelestai"* was stamped on the bill. Jesus had paid for our sins. He had paid in full.

DAY 21
THE CLEAN-UP: ABSOLUTION
LOOKING AT BOTH SIDES

THE ELEPHANT AND THE 6 BLIND MEN

There's an Indian parable about six blind men and an elephant, which has many versions. One version goes something like this:

There were once six blind men who came upon an elephant for the first time in their lives. The first man touched the elephant's trunk and said, "This animal is like a snake!"

The second man touched the tusk and said, "This animal is like a spear!"

The third man touched the knee and said, "This animal is like a tree!"

The fourth man touched the ear and said, "This animal is like a fan!"

The fifth man touched the side of the elephant and said, "This animal is like a wall!"

And the last man touched the tail and said, "This animal is like a rope!"

Every man was right, but they weren't describing the whole elephant. They were describing only one part of the animal. They were describing their own experience when they touched the elephant.

This parable teaches us that everyone has a different point of view on things. That's why listening to other views is an important part of learning to forgive.

HISTORY DETECTIVES

When historians want to discover something about the past, they look for evidence. A "primary source" is something that was written or created by the people who actually saw or experienced the event. It could be a photograph, diary, or letter.

However, these pieces of evidence often only tell a *part* of the story; therefore, historians have to put them all together like a puzzle to get the big picture. They're like detectives. They look at all of the evidence they can find to figure out what happened.

If we really want to clean up the mess after sin, we need to know the damage it caused. That means being like a historian or a detective and looking at all of the evidence of what happened. We need to consider all viewpoints.

For instance, some people in our country have not always had the same freedoms as everyone else. Racism is when you treat people differently depending on the color of their skin or what country they are from. When we think about the freedoms in our country, different groups will see things differently than others. African Americans, Native Americans, Chinese Americans, women, and young adults might view things differently because of their different experiences, such as with voting.

- In America in 1789, you could only vote if you were a man, owned property, and paid taxes. That was a very small percentage of people.
- In 1870, black men were allowed to vote.

- In 1920, women were allowed to vote.
- In 1924, all Native Americans were allowed to vote.
- In 1943, Chinese immigrants were allowed to become citizens and vote.
- In 1971, adults 18 years old and older were allowed to vote. Before then, you had to be at least 21.

If we don't understand different points of view, we will not be able to clean up the hurts caused by racism in our country. Jesus prayed, **"I am in them and you are in me. May they experience such perfect unity that the world will know that you sent me and that you love them as much as you love me." John 17:23 (NLT)**

JEWS, GENTILES, AND SAMARITANS

In Jesus's day, people also clashed over differences. But in the Book of Acts, we see how Jesus's message broke down dividing walls as it spread across the world.

The church began in Jerusalem, where most of the members were Jewish. Then, after Christians began to be persecuted, many fled from Jerusalem and took the Gospel to Gentiles (non-Jews) and Samaritans in Judea and Samaria. Jews and Samaritans had a history of conflict because Samaritans were Jews who had intermarried with non-believers many years before.

Finally, Paul took the Gospel even farther—"to the ends of the earth." As Paul said in Galatians 3:28, **"There is neither Jew nor Gentile, neither slave nor free, nor is there male and female, for you are all one in Christ Jesus."**

Meanwhile, Peter had this to say in Acts 10:34-35: **"I now realize how true it is that God does not show favoritism but accepts from every nation the one who fears him and does what is right."**

#FORGIVINGCHALLENGEKIDS

One of the names for Jesus is Prince of Peace. Even when Jesus was born, the angels' message was all about peace. A choir of angels sang this to the shepherds: **"Glory to God in highest heaven, and peace on earth to those with whom God is pleased" Luke 2:14 (NLT)**

With Jesus, we too can be peacemakers. We too can cross all sorts of barriers. It takes only that first step to begin.

CHALLENGE

Find a way to go to the "other side" by looking at something from another person's viewpoint.

1 **Check out a book from your local library on racial diversity.**
If you need some help, here are some recommendations:

- *It's OK to be Different,* by Sharon Purtill (diversity)
- *The Skin You Live In,* by Michael Tyler (acceptance)
- *Look What Brown Can Do!* by T. Marie Harris (black history)

2 **Learn about the history of another culture.**
Visit a culture fair or an international grocery store and try a new food!

3 **Stand up for what's right.**
Don't let others put down those who are different.

4 **Invite someone from a different culture to your house.**
Spending time with people who are different is the best way to learn about other cultures and different ways of doing things.

DAY 22
THE CLEAN-UP: ABSOLUTION
FORGIVENESS IS NOT A FEELING

CLEAN YOUR ROOM!
Look at the room below. Circle all of the things that are out of place.

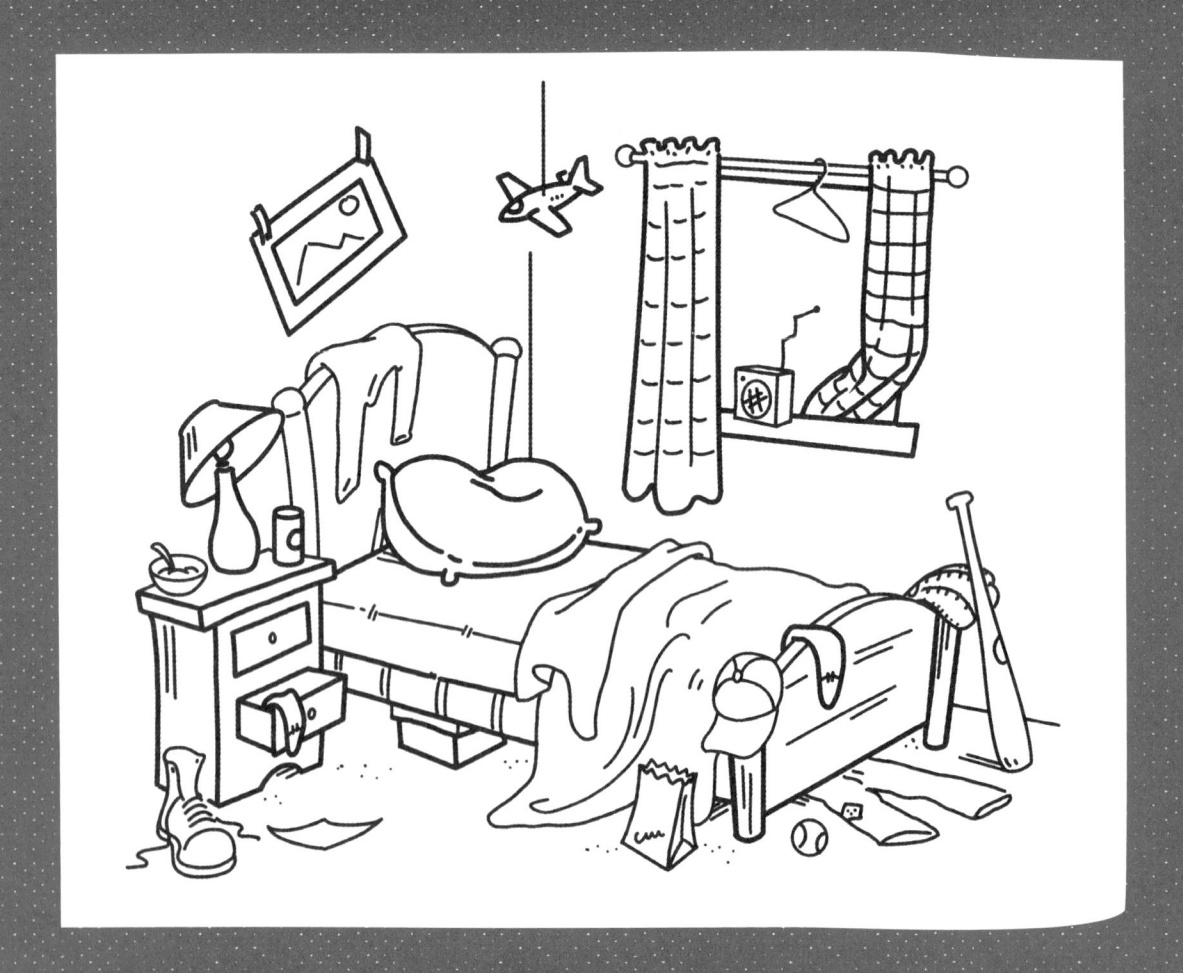

Do you have a clean-up song from home or one you sing at school? If not, give this one a try:

Clean up clean up,
Everybody everywhere,
Clean up clean up,
Everybody do your share.

Clean my room, Clean my room
At the end of day.
Pick my toys up one by one
and put them all away.

Some people are naturally neat and tidy, while others like to be more relaxed and go with the flow. What would you say you are?

☐ NEAT AND TIDY   ☐ RELAXED AND MESSY

(If you are interested in finding out more about your personality type, go to our website at **www.forgivingchallenge.com/personality** to take a personality test.)

Not everyone is a neat freak, but everyone has to clean up from time to time.

WHISTLE WHILE YOU WORK

One sign of growing up is learning to do things, such as cleaning your room and other chores, even when you don't feel like it. In the same way, you will not always feel like 'fessing up to your sins or cleaning up the messes you make with other people.

The disciple Peter knew he had to forgive, but he assumed that there had to be a limit. Here's what he asked Jesus: **"Master, how many times do I forgive a brother or sister who hurts me? Seven?" Jesus replied,** *"Seven! Hardly. Try seventy times seven."* **Matthew 18: 21-22 (The Message)**

Seventy times seven is 490 times! But when Jesus said we must forgive seventy times seven, He was not asking us to keep track of how many times we forgive

THE CLEAN-UP • 145

each other. "Okay, I hit 490, so I don't have to forgive anymore!" He didn't mean that. Jesus actually meant *infinity* when he said 490. Wow! That means there is no end to forgiveness. It's hard enough forgiving when you don't feel like it, but to be told that you have to forgive forever feels impossible.

FORGIVENESS IS A DECISION

The "seventy times seven" verse is not only about us. It's also about Jesus and what He's done. Jesus is telling us that His forgiveness for us is unlimited.

If you wrote down all of the bad things you did, it would be a lot more than 490. The debt of sin you owe is bigger than you can ever pay back. If Jesus didn't forgive us for this huge debt, we would all be prisoners for life.

In addition, Jesus did things even though He didn't always feel like it. Remember when we learned on Day 9 about Jesus praying in the Garden of Gethsemane? In the garden that night, he was praying that he wouldn't have to die on the cross. But Jesus accepted His Father's will, even when He didn't feel like it.

Forgiveness is more than a feeling. It is a decision. Not only are we forgiven, but the Bible says we are loved. Read the following verse about how strong this love is.

> "For I am convinced that neither death nor life, neither angels nor demons, neither the present nor the future, nor any powers, neither height nor depth, nor anything else in all creation, will be able to separate us from the love of God that is in Christ Jesus our Lord." Romans 8:38-39

You are loved more than you can ever imagine. God's love takes away the stain of sin and places a crown on your head. With a new, royal crown, you now have the power to 'fess up and clean up.

#FORGIVINGCHALLENGEKIDS

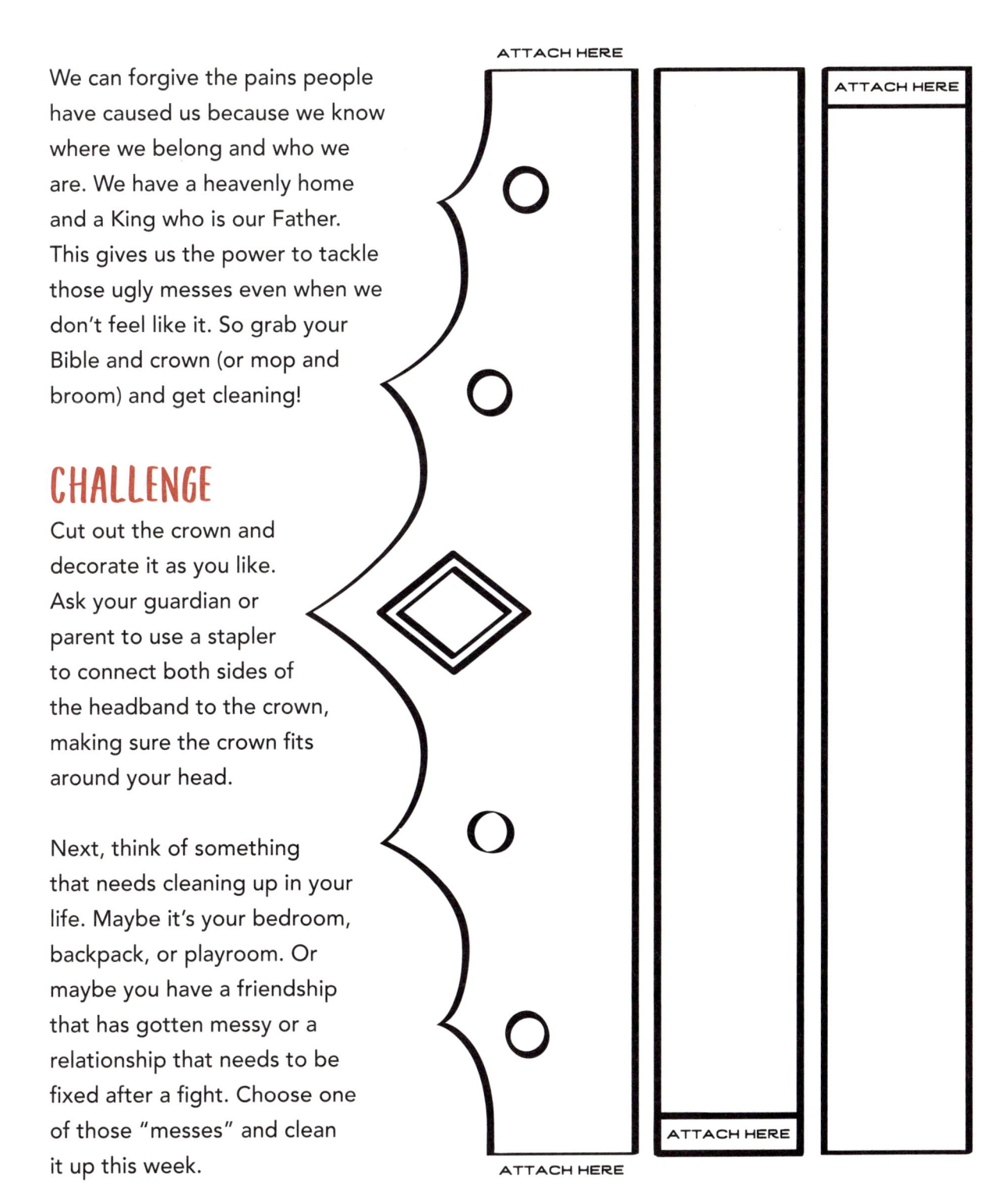

We can forgive the pains people have caused us because we know where we belong and who we are. We have a heavenly home and a King who is our Father. This gives us the power to tackle those ugly messes even when we don't feel like it. So grab your Bible and crown (or mop and broom) and get cleaning!

CHALLENGE

Cut out the crown and decorate it as you like. Ask your guardian or parent to use a stapler to connect both sides of the headband to the crown, making sure the crown fits around your head.

Next, think of something that needs cleaning up in your life. Maybe it's your bedroom, backpack, or playroom. Or maybe you have a friendship that has gotten messy or a relationship that needs to be fixed after a fight. Choose one of those "messes" and clean it up this week.

THE CLEAN-UP • 147

RED ALERT!

When runners in the ancient world won a race, they received a crown made out of myrtle plants. We too will receive a crown as followers of Jesus. But Paul says our crown will not decay like a plant. It will last and shine forever (1 Corinthians 9:25).

#FORGIVINGCHALLENGEKIDS

DAY 23
THE CLEAN-UP: ABSOLUTION
WHEN HATE CLOUDS OUR MINDS

THE ROOF OF THE WORLD

There are only 14 mountains on Earth with peaks over 26,247 feet high, and you'll find 10 of those enormous mountains in the Himalayas. That is why this incredible mountain range is referred to as the "Roof of the World."

Anything above 26,000 feet on a mountain is called the "death zone." People could not survive there without additional oxygen. Because Mount Everest rises 29,032 feet high, you need oxygen to reach the top.

The air this high is called "thin" because it contains less oxygen. But when you get up into this thin air, even with oxygen tanks, you can begin to have side effects from low oxygen. You may feel restless, not be able to recognize people or speak clearly, and some people even have illusions and see things that are not there.

In climbing the mountain of forgiveness, hate can make you feel a lot like that. The hate you feel for someone who hurt you may cloud your mind and keep you from speaking or thinking clearly. You may even start to remember things differently and see things that are not there.

THE DEN OF ROBBERS

It's important to remember the difference between hate and anger. It is normal and natural to be angry when someone hurts you. That anger will go away as you heal.

We also know anger is okay because the Bible says that Jesus got angry. One day, Jesus went to the Temple, where he saw people using it like a market. They were selling cows, sheep, and doves, taking advantage of people to make money. They were not in the Temple to worship God, so Jesus became very angry. He tipped over tables and used a whip to drive people out.

> "It is written," **he said to them,** "'My house will be called a house of prayer,' but you are making it 'a den of robbers.'" Matthew 21:13

Jesus didn't hate. He wanted to correct the situation and make it better. Hating only makes things worse.

ANGER OR HATRED?

Hate festers and spreads, killing everything good in its path. Without some hard work, hate can get out of control. If you want to check whether you're feeling anger or hate, ask yourself: "What would make these feelings go away?"

- If you just want to correct the problem, then your anger will die when things are resolved.
- If you desire to cause harm or trouble to the other person even when things are worked out, then you may have some hate in your heart.

It is okay to admit those feelings, because then we can get help. Like the death zone on a mountain, those feelings signal a danger zone for your mind and heart.

If climbers never admitted when they were feeling dizzy or different, they would not get to the summit of the mountain. They would be stuck.

Hate can leave us stuck in the journey of forgiveness because hate focuses on the person, and not the thing they did. The strange thing is that the more you love someone, the easier you will find it is to hate them for things they do. Scientists used a brain scanner to discover that where you feel hate and where you feel love come from the exact same place in the brain.

> **"Make a clean break with all cutting, backbiting, profane talk. Be gentle with one another, sensitive. Forgive one another as quickly and thoroughly as God in Christ forgave you." Ephesians 4:31- 32 (The Message)**

So clear your mind of hate and take a deep breath. The air is sweet.

CHALLENGE

There are many ways you can climb out of the pit of hate. When you need to deal with your hatred, practice the three 'Rs'—Remember, Refocus, and Record:

1 **REMEMBER** the action someone did, and be upset at that, instead of at the person. Below, write down several "actions" and the persons involved. Then be mad at the actions.

ACTION	PERSON
_____	_____
_____	_____
_____	_____
_____	_____

#FORGIVINGCHALLENGEKIDS

2 **REFOCUS** by praying for the person. You cannot hate someone you are praying for. God can melt your hurting heart, and you will find the hate will slowly shrink until it's gone. Hate has to be fed to stay alive.

3 **RECORD** how you felt. Sometimes remembering what you like about a person can help you overcome the hate.

_____
_____
_____
_____
_____

RED ALERT!

When Jesus drove the "moneychangers" from the Temple, that's sometimes called "the cleansing of the Temple." So Jesus was very good at "clean-ups." Moneychangers exchanged foreign money for coins that could be used in Jerusalem. But they often cheated people.

DAY 24

THE CLEAN-UP: ABSOLUTION

DON'T HIDE FROM YOUR PROBLEMS

NO HIDING UNDER BUSHELS

Have you ever been asked to clean up your room and instead you just shoved everything out of sight? Clothes get crammed into drawers, all sports equipment is squished into the closet, and cluttered toys on the floor are jammed under the bed.

At first glance, your room might look picked up, but you'd find out pretty soon that it's very difficult to live in a room like that. Imagine such a room while you read the story below.

THE PERPETUAL PIGSTY

When you open your drawer (if you can even get it open) to get dressed in the morning, you can't tell which clothes are clean and which are dirty. After a quick sniff test, you determine that one rumpled T-shirt doesn't smell too bad, so you put it on. Then you go over to the closet to get out your soccer ball, but you can't find it in the gigantic pile. You're afraid to start digging, because everything will come crashing down.

Never mind. You'll play *Monopoly*, your favorite board game, instead. You find the box stuck far beneath your bed, but the pieces, cards, and money are scattered all over your room. It would be impossible to play without actually cleaning up your room. So forget about any games.

Finally, you give up and go outside. Who wants to spend time in a mess like that?

Sometimes, we deal with our problems the same way. Instead of facing our problems and trying to fix them, we push all of our hurt feelings and disappointments out of sight. We think that if we can just cram them deep enough, like the clothes in our drawers, then maybe we won't have to deal with them. Out of sight, out of mind.

Pretending our problems don't exist is a big problem. If you're not careful, things can come crashing down on you like an overstuffed closet.

HIDE AND SEEK

Even the disciples wanted to hide when things got rough. When Jesus died, the disciples believed their mission was over. They were also afraid that they too might be killed, so they hid in fear. They crammed into a room all together and locked the door. They thought hiding would keep them safe.

But doors and walls didn't keep Jesus out! He walked right through them and brought light into a dark room. John tells us that after Jesus appeared to them, one of the first things He talked about was forgiveness.

> **"Then he took a deep breath and breathed into them.** 'Receive the Holy Spirit,' **he said.** 'If you forgive someone's sins, they're gone for good. If you don't forgive sins, what are you going to do with them?'"
> **John 20: 22-23 (The Message)**

Trying to hide our feelings is not the same as forgiveness. Forgiveness does not squish troubles back into the darkness. Forgiveness brings everything into the light.

Jesus says He is the light of the world. And if He can walk through walls to find the disciples, He can come through the doors of our hearts, even if we've locked them. Jesus brings in the shining light of His forgiveness.

As Jesus once said, **"I am the world's Light. No one who follows me stumbles around in the darkness. I provide plenty of light to live in." John 8:12 (The Message)**

A TOTAL CHANGE

The disciples went from being scaredy cats, hiding in the darkness, to the most courageous preachers in history. If you read the Book of Acts, you'll see that they kept getting arrested—and kept going back to the Temple to preach about Jesus. Even after the disciples were each lashed 39 times and thrown into prison, an angel got them out in the night. The next morning, they were back at the Temple preaching.

What a 180-degree change! There was no explanation for the dramatic change in them, except for the power of God. Historians say this is a sign that Jesus's resurrection was real.

It takes courage to recognize our sins, confess them, and then try to fix things. No sin is too large that Jesus's death and resurrection cannot pay for it, so don't worry. You can bring all of that mess out into the open. He can take care of it. He's got a big mop.

#FORGIVINGCHALLENGEKIDS

CHALLENGE

Look up the lyrics to the song "In the Light" by dc Talk online, or find the song on YouTube and listen to it. Use it as a time of prayer and think about the words. What is the song saying about God's light?

_____
_____
_____
_____
_____
_____

RED ALERT!

Peter and the disciples received a common punishment in Bible days—"40 lashes minus one." Because it would be disgraceful to exceed 40 lashes, the court gave people 39, just in case they miscounted.

DAY 25
THE CLEAN-UP: ABSOLUTION
FORGIVING IS NOT FORGETTING

REMEMBER THIS!

Test your memory. Give yourself two minutes to memorize as many of the items below as you can. Then, without looking at the pictures, write down all of the items you remember.

How many did you remember? _____ out of 20.

MEMORY LANE

Have you ever heard someone say, "Just forget about it," when you apologize? Does this mean forgiveness is just another word for forgetting?

It's not.

You can't forgive something you have forgotten. But hold on, you might say. Doesn't the Bible talk about God forgetting our sin? For instance, the prophet Isaiah describes God's forgiveness this way: **"I, even I, am he who blots out your transgressions, for my own sake, and remembers your sins no more." Isaiah 43:25**

When the Bible says that God will remember your sins no more, that does not mean He has one of His angels use a memory eraser thingy and POOF! God's memory is wiped clean. What this means is that when God forgives you, He is choosing to not treat you the way you deserve.

> **"God is sheer mercy and grace;**
> **   not easily angered, he's rich in love.**
> **He doesn't endlessly nag and scold,**
> **   nor hold grudges forever.**
> **He doesn't treat us as our sins deserve,**
> **   nor pay us back in full for our wrongs."**
> **Psalm 103:8-9 (The Message)**

In fact, God says that when the Israelites mess up and 'fess up, when they sin and confess, He will remember. He will remember their covenant (a promise or agreement).

Leviticus 26:40a, 41b-42 of *The Message* puts it this way:

> **"On the other hand, if they confess their sins and the sins of their ancestors…if by some chance they soften their hard hearts and make amends for their sin, I'll remember my covenant with Jacob, I'll remember my covenant with Isaac, and, yes, I'll remember my covenant with Abraham. And I'll remember the land."**

Instead of memory-erasing, God took our sin and placed it on Jesus. Because of His death on the cross, Jesus was able to remove our sins as far as the east is from the west. He gives us the power to forgive what we remember.

Don't forget that.

CHALLENGE

Go outside right now (bring your book with you!) and look to the eastern horizon. Hint: The east is where the sun rises. Now look to the western horizon. The west is where the sun sets every evening. God says that this is how far He has removed our sins from us—as far as the east is from the west.

Imagine being able to sail up out of the earth's atmosphere, past the moon, past our solar system and even past our Milky Way galaxy. God has removed your sin and the sin of others even farther away than that!

To help you remember how much you have been forgiven, your challenge today is to memorize Psalm 103:11-12. Use the following hand gestures to help you!

#FORGIVINGCHALLENGEKIDS

For as high as the heavens are above the earth,
  (STRETCH YOUR ARMS WAY UP HIGH.)

so great is his love for those who fear him;
  (HUG YOUR ARMS AROUND YOURSELF.)

as far as the east is from the west,
  (STRETCH YOUR ARMS OUT FAR APART.)

so far has he removed our transgressions from us.
  (PUSH YOUR ARMS IN FRONT OF YOU.)

RED ALERT!

The Old Covenant is the law, which the Bible calls "holy, righteous, and good" (Romans 7:12). But we cannot be saved by the law. That's why Jesus came to bring the New Covenant—the new promise. The New Covenant brings forgiveness when we fail to live up to the law.

DAY 26
THE CLEAN-UP: ABSOLUTION
GOD ERASES ALL OF OUR SINS

'DECORATING' CARS AND WALLS

One day, a little girl took a pointy rock and looked around for something to use it to draw on. Her eyes fell on the shiny family car.

As she drew on the car, the rock was so sharp that it took off the paint and left a permanent message on the side of her dad's car. Although the father was upset, he could not punish the little girl when he saw it. Here's what the message said:

Did you ever "decorate" your walls as a kid? Many children have used a crayon, marker, or even a Sharpie to draw some beautiful pictures on their parents' walls. Then their parents have to scrub, wash, or paint over the marks.

Ask your parents if there was a time you ever "decorated" something that wasn't supposed to be colored on. What did you do?

_____

_____

MARKS ON OUR HEARTS

Sin is kind of like that rock or marker. It carves permanent scars into our hearts that cannot be erased with a sponge or magic eraser. No matter how much you scrub, the marks will never be removed.

When it comes to forgiving others, we may try to make it right. Maybe we pay for the item we broke, or we do a favor for someone we hurt. Maybe we say, "I love you," to show we are no longer mad.

But we can't make things right on our own power. We can't scrub off the scars that sin left. They are too deep. We must be washed clean by a power outside of ourselves—by God.

> **"Have mercy upon me, O God, according to Your lovingkindness; according to the multitude of Your tender mercies, blot out my transgressions. Wash me thoroughly from my iniquity, and cleanse me from my sin." Psalm 51:1-2 (NKJV)**

NO SIN TOO BIG TO BE FORGIVEN

Before we can forgive others, we must first understand what God has done for us and how He sees us.

In *The Lion, the Witch and the Wardrobe*, by C.S. Lewis, a boy named Edmund made some bad mistakes that he could not fix on his own. When his accuser, the Witch, calls him a traitor in front of the great king, Aslan, she is right.

"You have a traitor there, Aslan," said the Witch. Of course everyone present knew that she meant Edmund. But Edmund had got past thinking about himself after all he'd been through and after the talk he'd had that morning. He just went on looking at Aslan. It didn't seem to matter what the Witch said.

When we understand what Jesus did for us, it doesn't matter what Satan or others call us, even if they are right. Like Edmund, we just keep looking at Jesus. There is no scrape too deep, no mark too dark, and no sin too big that Jesus's death cannot erase it.

It isn't magic. It's Jesus.

CHALLENGE

Write an invisible message, something like "Jesus can erase any sin." Here's how to do that:

1. Take two pieces of paper. Soak one completely in water. Keep the other one dry.

2. Place the dry piece of paper on top of the wet paper. Then use a pen to write a message ON THE DRY PAPER, pressing hard with the pen. This will "press" the message into the wet paper below.

3. Set the wet paper aside and let it dry. The "pressed-in" message will disappear when the paper dries.

4. To make the invisible message reappear, dip the paper in water or soak it thoroughly. You should be able to read it once again.

#FORGIVINGCHALLENGEKIDS

RED ALERT!

Death entered the world through the sin of Adam. But resurrection life entered the world through Jesus (1 Corinthians 15:21-22). That's why the Bible calls Jesus the "last Adam."

#FORGIVINGCHALLENGEKIDS

DAYS 27-33
OF THE 40-DAY CHALLENGE

THE RISE-UP:
RESTO

RATION

HAVE FUN COLORING THIS PAGE!
FIND MORE LIKE THIS AT FORGIVINGCHALLENGE.COM/KIDS

THE MOUNTAINS OF REDVALE

PART 5

As the group began the long trudge back up the inside of the volcano, Malachi slipped beside Isabella. "What's troubling you?" he asked. Malachi had an uncanny way of sensing when she was bothered by something.

"I'm happy that Emily and Aiden made peace with Frankie and Chloe. I really am," she said. "But I wish I could make things right with Nova, and I don't know if that's ever going to be possible. I'm afraid our friendship is broken for good."

"Repairing a friendship is like mending a broken bone," Malachi said. "It doesn't happen overnight. But given the right care, your friendship can heal."

"But what if Nova doesn't even want to fix our friendship?"

"That is a risk. You can't control her response, but you can pray about it."

"But I'm not just worried about Nova," Isabella said. "I also want to forgive the kids who've been teasing me on TikTok and Clubhouse, but I don't know a lot of them. How do I forgive someone I don't even know? And how can I stop feeling so angry? Am I a bad person for feeling angry?"

"Anger isn't always bad," Malachi said. "Jesus got angry with the money-changers who were ripping off people in the Temple courts. The question is: Are you trapped in your anger?"

"Trapped?"

"Yes. Like the sticky slime that trapped Frankie and Chloe. When you're stuck in your anger, it takes over your life."

"But—"

Before Isabella could complete her thought, Red let out a shout. "Hey, these rocks weren't here when we came down this way!" The little fox pointed at a huge pile of rocks blocking the path leading upward.

"A landslide must've happened, but don't worry. There's a second way to the top," Malachi said, turning around and leading them back to a different path. "This way is a little longer and a little more dangerous, but we have no choice."

"Did he just say this path is a little more dangerous?" Frankie whispered to Aiden. "How 'little' is a little more dangerous?"

"We better pick up the pace!" Red shouted, running up ahead of Malachi and Isabella. "We foxes have pretty good ears, and I'm picking up an increase in the gurgling sound coming from down below."

"And donkeys like me have a pretty good sense of smell," Balthazar added. "The smell of slime is increasing."

Malachi and the others peered back down into the bottom of the volcano. Red and Balthazar were right. Green slime was beginning to bubble up the central shaft of the mountain.

"Watch out!" Isabella shouted, as a stream of green slime suddenly appeared on the path behind them. Being gooey, the slime wasn't racing toward them, but they still had to move fast to stay ahead of it.

"Oh man, oh man, I don't wanna get stuck in that stuff again," Frankie said, elbowing his way through the group and pushing his way in front of everyone.

"Hey, watch what you're doing!" Aiden said. He caught up to Frankie and gave him a shove from behind. Then Emily and Chloe leaped into the tussle, and pretty soon all four of the kids were shoving and shouting.

"Guys, guys, guys!" Red shouted, dancing around them. "We're never going to stay ahead of the slime if you keep fighting!"

Frankie gave another slug to Aiden's shoulder and then rushed ahead before Aiden could punch back. The way ahead was a narrow, twisting, rocky path. Suddenly, the volcano gave out a big belch and a blob of green slime flew into the air and came down on Frankie's head.

"Ah! Get it off! Get it off!"

#FORGIVINGCHALLENGEKIDS

The volcano gave out a second belch, sending two big blobs into the air. One just missed Isabella and the other got stuck on a stalactite hanging from the ceiling like a stone dagger.

The mountain was angry, and they still had a long, long way to go.

THE ROCKTOPUS

Aiden was furious. When they had made peace with Frankie and Chloe, he thought the two bullies had changed. But Frankie was up to his old tricks. He was still pushy and loud and always looking to get his own way.

Aiden's legs were aching at the strain as he and Frankie led the way up the steep path. They kept trying to shove in front of each other. Whenever Aiden got in front, Frankie reached out, grabbed his shirt, and yanked him back.

"Stop it!" he shouted, taking hold of Frankie's shirt and pulling him backward.

Finally, Malachi put his foot down. He decided that Balthazar would go to the front of the line and lead them up the path, while Aiden and Frankie would have to stay back, preferably far apart from one another.

Aiden decided to walk beside Malachi, who remained at the back of the pack to keep an eye on them.

"I don't get it," Aiden said softly so Frankie couldn't hear. "Frankie doesn't seem to be any different. I thought we had made peace."

"Do you think people completely change their personality just because you make peace with them?" Malachi said.

"I thought he'd at least change some."

"Maybe he has, but you can't see it. Besides, you're not called to forgive just so the other person has a change of heart. You forgive to change YOUR heart."

Just then, Balthazar came to a halt, and the entire line stopped. "Malachi, you've got to see this."

Balthazar nodded his head in the direction of yet another big rock blocking the path. But there was something odd about this boulder. It almost looked like it had two closed eyes in the front.

THE MOUNTAINS OF REDVALE • 171

"If that's what I think it is, be very, very careful," Malachi said. "We don't want to wake it. This might be a Rocktopus."

"A Rocktopus? You mean that rock is alive?" Chloe asked.

"Oh yes. Very much alive. But maybe we can slip past without waking it."

Malachi put a finger to his lips and walked softly up to the boulder, which was about five feet wide. There was barely room on the left side of the path to slip by. Malachi motioned for Aiden to sneak past the Rocktopus next.

As Aiden edged closer and closer to the creature, he thought he could hear it breathing heavily. *Careful now,* he told himself as he edged to the left of the rock. *Easy…easy…*

"GOOD MORNING, REDVALE!" The boulder's eyes suddenly shot open, as if somebody had turned on a switch. Aiden leaped backward, smashing his back against a wall of rock.

"HELLO, HELLO, HELLO!" the boulder shouted, and eight long, stony arms shot from his side. He extended one of the arms, seeming to want to shake hands.

"He seems friendly enough," Emily said.

"OF COURSE I'M FRIENDLY! I'M THE FRIENDLIEST ROCK IN THIS ENTIRE VOLCANO! WON'T YOU BE MY NEIGHBOR? LET'S SHAKE HANDS!"

The Rocktopus was also the loudest rock in the entire volcano. He spoke every word like a mighty shout. And when Emily smiled at him, the Rocktopus directed his arm at her.

"SHAKE HANDS, LITTLE MISSIE!"

"No, don't!" Malachi shouted, stepping between Emily and the boulder.

"Why not? He just wants to make friends."

"Rocktopuses don't make friends," Malachi said. "He wants to grab you."

At these words, the Rocktopus changed in an instant—again, as if somebody flipped a switch.

"ARE YOU CALLING ME UNFRIENDLY? NOBODY CALLS ME UNFRIENDLY AND LIVES TO TALK ABOUT IT!"

#FORGIVINGCHALLENGEKIDS

The Rocktopus tried to smack Malachi with one of his eight flailing hands. But Malachi was too quick, and he used his staff to block the creature's attack.

"I WILL, I WILL ROCK YOU!" the boulder bellowed.

The boulder lunged forward, but it didn't roll. It almost seemed to glide. When Malachi poked the Rocktopus with his staff, the boulder immediately came to a stop. His expression changed in an instant.

"I'm so sorry, so very, very, very, very, very sorry!" the Rocktopus lamented. "I feel so bad. Whatever can I do to make this up to you?"

"Do you mean it?" Isabella asked.

In response, the boulder made another instant switch. He displayed anger once again. "OF COURSE I MEAN IT, YOU FOOL! DO YOU DARE TO QUESTION ME?"

"Back!" Malachi shouted, poking the boulder with his staff. The boulder used another hand to wipe his eyes, where water trickled down like a spring. The boulder seemed to be weeping.

"You don't like me," the boulder sobbed. "Nobody likes me! I try to be nice, but nobody is nice back!"

"Who knew that rocks could be so emotional?" Chloe said, giving Emily a nudge.

"That's exactly right," Malachi said, taking one step back. "Rocktopuses switch between eight different emotions, as fast as flipping through channels with your TV remote. Eight arms and eight emotions. So far, we've seen joy, anger, guilt, and sadness."

"This rock needs to chill," Frankie said.

"What did you just say?" the Rocktopus asked, looking around in panic. "I need to chill? But I'm not hot, so why do I need to chill! Or am I warm to the touch? Do I have a fever? Am I sick? I think I'm sick. Maybe I'm dying. What's wrong with me?"

"He's moved on to feelings of worry," Malachi said.

Malachi's words triggered another change in the Rocktopus. "You guys are really beginning to bug me," the boulder said. "First you call me unfriendly. Then you tell me I'm a worrier."

"Now he's moved to the feeling of frustration," Malachi said.

"I want to attack you, but I'm not sure if I can defeat all of you," added the boulder.

"And now he's filled with doubt."

Suddenly, the boulder glided away from the kids, his eyes going wide with alarm.

"GET AWAY FROM ME! GET AWAY! LEAVE ME ALONE!"

"And there's the eighth emotion," said Malachi. "Fear."

"If he's afraid of us, that's good, isn't it?" Emily said.

Suddenly, the boulder looked fierce and swung wildly at Emily, nearly whacking her with one of his long, rocky arms. Emily jumped back just in time.

"HOW DARE YOU CALL ME AFRAID! I'M NOT AFRAID OF ANYONE!"

"Back to anger," Isabella said. "How do we get him to stay afraid of us—at least until we can get by him?"

"Uh…guys, you better think of a way to get past this boulder soon," Frankie said. "Look behind us."

Aiden turned and saw the stream of green slime moving up the slope, gurgling and giving off a horrible stench. If they didn't figure out how to get past the boulder, they were going to be trapped in goo.

"I think each arm triggers a different emotion," Malachi said. "I just need to figure out which one is the 'fear arm.'" Using his staff, he tapped one of the arms, and the boulder broke down sobbing.

"Nope. That's sadness."

Malachi poked a second arm with his staff.

"I really feel bad about causing you guys so many problems," the boulder moaned. "I wish I could move out of your path, but I just can't, and I feel truly awful about it."

#FORGIVINGCHALLENGEKIDS

"I think that's guilt. Try that arm," Emily said, pointing at one of the arms flailing about.

But when Malachi tapped that arm, the boulder erupted. "HOW DARE YOU TOUCH ME! HOW DARE YOU! I AM GOING TO CRUSH YOU!"

"No, that's anger," Malachi said, as the boulder moved in on them, driving them back toward the steadily approaching slime. The slime was only about ten feet away, closing fast.

"Do something!"

Malachi tapped another one of the Rocktopus's arms. No use. It created worries once again. But then, just as the slime was about two feet from reaching Aiden, Malachi struck the bottom of the four left arms with his staff.

"Get away from me! Get away! Get away!" the boulder shouted.

That was the one! F*ear.*

As the Rocktopus glided backward, they moved forward as a group, trying to stay one step ahead of the goo. Before the creature could switch to another emotion, Malachi used his staff to poke the arm that triggered fear. He kept poking it, again and again and again. The terrified boulder kept moving backward.

"Don't do that! You're scaring me! You're really scaring me!"

Aiden almost felt a little sorry for the poor boulder. But they had no choice. As the boulder retreated in terror, they pressed forward, with the slime close at their heels. Finally, the Rocktopus got so scared that it turned and glided away, disappearing into a cave.

"Let's move!" Malachi shouted.

The slime was only inches away from Aiden's shoe when the path finally became clear, and he sprinted ahead. He and Frankie continued to fight to get to the front, elbowing and pushing every step of the way.

A BRIDGE OVER TROUBLED GOO

"You know, I'm getting a little tired of Frankie and Aiden constantly fighting," Chloe said to Emily, as the group pressed on.

"I'm sick of it too," Emily said. "Aiden always has to be first in everything."

"Frankie is just the same way!" Chloe exclaimed. "He has to win every game of Monopoly."

"Aiden has to win every game of checkers."

"And Frankie has to turn everything into a race or contest."

"Aiden does too. He even tries to see who can brush their teeth the fastest!"

Chloe smiled, and Emily realized she wasn't so bad after all.

"I'm glad you two are getting along so well," said Malachi, coming up behind them.

"We're finding we have more in common than we thought," said Emily.

"Yeah. *Pesky brothers!*"

Emily and Chloe broke out laughing.

"Are all Rocktopuses like that—so emotional?" Chloe asked Malachi, after she finally controlled her giggling.

"Sadly, yes," said Malachi. "They're controlled by their emotions, constantly swinging from one feeling to another."

"Sounds tiring," Emily said.

"It is. That's why they sleep a lot."

"I worry sometimes," Chloe said. "Is it bad to worry?"

"No, it's what you do with your feelings that's important," Malachi said. "Some people try to ignore their feelings, and other people let out all of their feelings—like the Rocktopus. I prefer the third way."

"What's that?"

"Be open about your feelings but not controlled by them. Take your feelings to God."

"Oh," said Chloe.

Emily could sense that Chloe didn't want to talk about God. Malachi must've also sensed the same thing because he decided to leave them be. He rushed ahead to try to bring peace between Frankie and Aiden.

#FORGIVINGCHALLENGEKIDS

Emily and Chloe walked on in silence. Emily, being a talker, couldn't take the silence any longer. So she asked Chloe, "What do you worry about?"

Chloe didn't answer.

"I'm sorry. I can be too nosy sometimes."

"No, no, that's okay," said Chloe. "I just never had anyone ask me before. But…well, I guess I worry the most about whether other kids will like me."

That's odd, Emily thought. *If Chloe worried so much about kids not liking her, then why was she such a bully? That's the worst way to get people to like you.*

"I guess that's why I pick on other kids," Chloe said, as if answering the question in Emily's mind. "If I give them a good reason not to like me, then I won't worry about them liking me."

"Oh. I think I understand."

"But everyone seems to like you," said Chloe. "I suppose that's why I pick on you the most. How do you get people to like you?"

"Talking with them is a good way to start. Like we're doing. And I have to say, Chloe. I do think you're nice."

"Really? After all I've done to you?"

"That's in the past. I'm talking about *now.*"

Chloe beamed. Emily never knew she had such a nice smile. Come to think of it, today might be the first day Chloe ever smiled at her.

"What kind of things do you like to do the most?" Emily asked, trying to keep the conversation going.

"That's easy. I like animals. We have two dogs, three cats, a gerbil, a parakeet, and an iguana."

"An iguana! That's so cool! I love animals too!"

"Did somebody say they love animals?" Red chirped, popping up beside them. "I love animals too!"

"That's because you are one," said Emily.

"Yeah, but he's a *talking* animal! Chloe said. "Is Redvale the coolest land or what?"

For the next twenty minutes, Chloe, Emily, and Red chatted about training dogs, feeding iguanas, and the age at which talking foxes in Redvale learn to speak. By the end of it, Chloe was carrying Red on top of her shoulders, and the talkative fox was telling her all about how many languages he knew.

It was a grand time…at least until they reached a stone bridge over a great chasm. The bridge, only about five feet wide, arched across the open space. It had no railings. Nothing. Emily figured that this must be what Malachi meant by the path being "a little more dangerous."

"Is this our only way to the top?" she asked.

"I'm afraid so," Malachi said. "But if we stay close together, we—"

Before Malachi could even complete his sentence, Frankie bolted for the bridge and began bragging, "I'm not afraid. I'll be the first to cross!"

But as Frankie stepped onto the bridge, Aiden was right behind, pulling him back and shouting, "In your dreams! I'll be the first to cross."

Furious, Malachi made a move to grab them both by the collars, but the two boys were too quick. In a flash, Frankie and Aiden were partway across the bridge, still tussling over who would be the first one across.

"This bridge is not designed to carry such anger!" Malachi said.

Sure enough, the bridge began to crumble beneath Frankie and Aiden's feet. Malachi reached out with his staff and told them to grab on. As the portion of the bridge beneath their feet turned to dust, Frankie latched on to the staff, and Aiden grabbed on to Frankie. But they couldn't hold on. It's much harder than it looks in the movies.

To their horror, Frankie lost his grip, and the two boys tumbled into the void below.

TO BE CONTINUED ON PAGE 208.

#FORGIVINGCHALLENGEKIDS

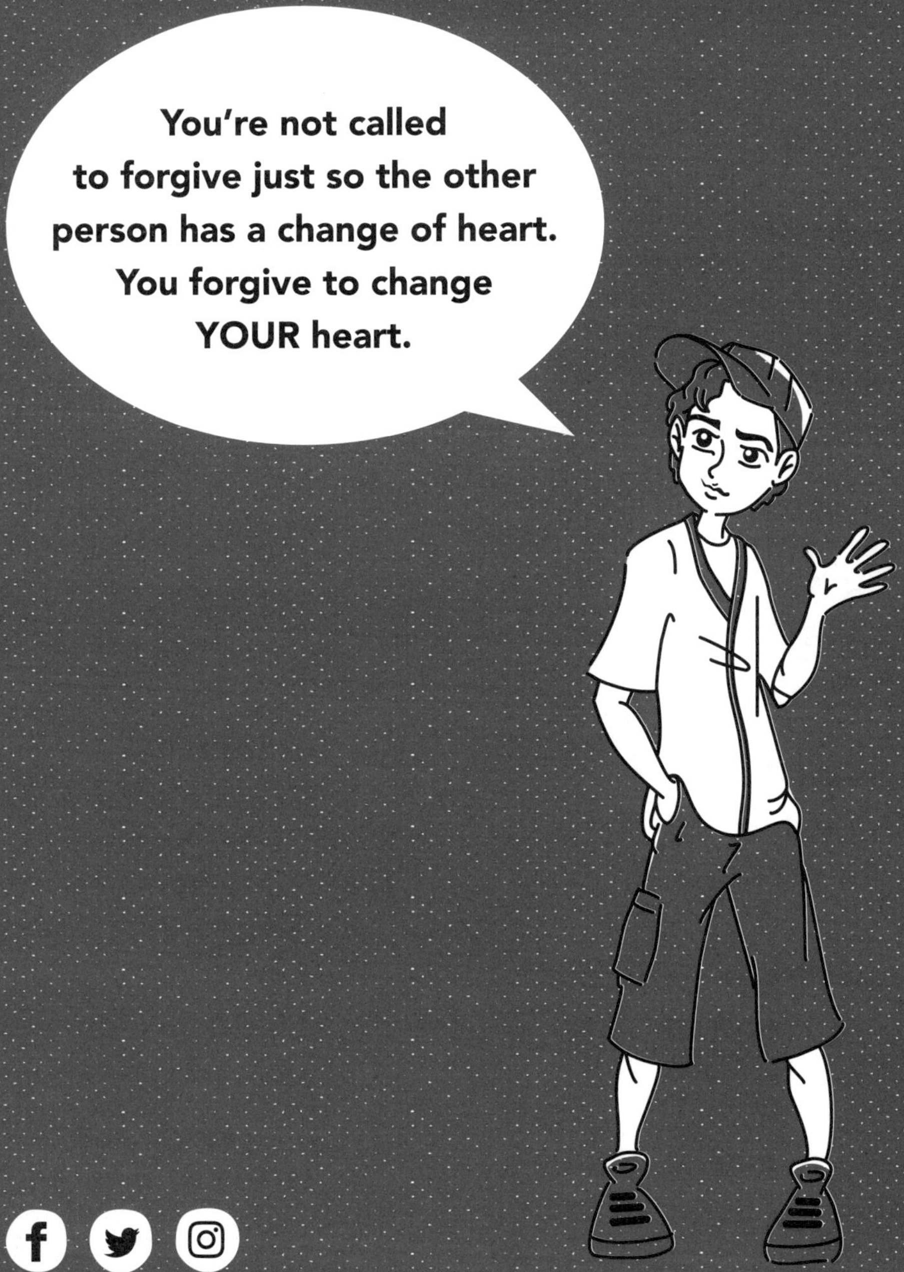

#FORGIVINGCHALLENGEKIDS

DAY 27
THE RISE-UP: RESTORATION
FORGIVENESS IS CREATIVE

LEGOS AND BROKEN BONES

If you put together a brand-new Lego set, what are you more likely to do:

1. Put it on display on a shelf?
2. Play with it until it breaks apart and then build something new?

Like a Lego set, forgiveness is picking up the old pieces and putting them back together again. It's a creative process, as it says in the book of Galatians.

> "Live creatively, friends. If someone falls into sin, forgivingly restore him, saving your critical comments for yourself. You might be needing forgiveness before the day's out." Galatians 6:1-2 (The Message)

Forgiveness is also like fixing a broken bone. In fact, the word "restore" means to reset, like a broken bone that needs to be put back into place. When a bone breaks, you don't remove it from the body. You can't live without your bones! Instead, you restore the bone to its original condition. You do this by setting the broken bone back in its original position, so it will heal properly.

In the same way, when hurts happen, usually the answer is not to remove the relationship from your life completely. God wants us to restore the relationship and put things back together in their proper place. God wants us to be creative, rather than just throwing away our relationship.

PUTTING THE PIECES BACK TOGETHER

During this week, we will be talking about how we RISE UP after we CLEAN UP our mess. Like a broken bone, this can take many weeks, even months, to heal. To forgive, you make something new.

The most creative being in the world is God. And since you are made in God's image, you can be part of that creativity. Creativity means having the power or ability to make something new. When you forgive, you are bringing life back into a relationship. If someone hurts you, it doesn't take any creativity to get revenge. Getting even disintegrates things and breaks people apart, like a smashed Lego set. It's the opposite of creative.

In many other religions, people must follow a set of rules to earn the right to be with their god. But the true God forgives us and mends our brokenness, rather than tossing us aside when we sin.

God made each and every one of us, so He knows how to put us back together. He has the M.I.M., or Master Instruction Manual, and no person is so broken that God cannot put him or her back together. The Good News of Jesus changes us from the inside out and restores us again, shiny and new. In *The Lego Movie*, the theme song was called "Everything is Awesome." In real life, of course, everything is not awesome. But when Jesus makes us new, THAT is truly awesome.

CHALLENGE

Build something with Legos or blocks today. As you build, think about how God will take all of the broken things of this world and restore them again one day.

DAY 28
THE RISE-UP: RESTORATION
FORGIVENESS TAKES TIME

THE SURVIVOR TREE

On Day 12, you learned about the horrible tragedy that happened on September 11, 2001, when terrorists crashed two planes into the World Trade Center In New York City. If you visit that spot today, you'll see a monument built to honor those who died. And in the middle of the courtyard is a pear tree. It is a true survivor of 9/11.

When the Twin Towers fell, all of the other trees around were burned or crushed. Only one little stump of the pear tree was left alive. That tree stump was saved and sent to a tree nursery where it grew new branches. Finally, after nine years, the pear tree was planted back at the site where the Twin Towers fell. The pear tree's beautiful white blossoms are a sign of hope in a place where so much hurt happened.

Nine years may seem like a long time to wait for healing, but for two brothers in the Bible, forgiveness took much longer than that.

BATTLE OF THE BLESSING

Jacob and Esau were twin brothers, but they were not identical twins. In fact, they were as different as you can get. Esau was a hairy man who liked to hunt. Jacob, his younger brother (by a few seconds), was more of a homebody.

Because Esau was older, common law said he deserved what is called the "birthright" from his father. The birthright gave the older brother certain honors. For instance, it made the older brother the family leader, and it gave him a "double portion" of the inheritance—twice as much as other brothers.

Jacob talked Esau into trading his birthright for a bowl of soup. (Esau was really hungry when he made that crazy trade.) Although Esau gave up his birthright, he could still receive the special blessing given to the oldest son. But Jacob, the young schemer, had a trick up his sleeve.

As the Bible tells the story in Genesis 27, their father, Isaac, was very old and getting ready to die when it was time to give the blessing to Esau. Rebecca, their mother, helped Jacob fool his dad by tying animal fur on his body so he felt hairy and smelled like Esau.

Because Isaac could not see well, he thought Jacob was Esau, and so he gave his blessing to Jacob. Once a father gives a blessing, it cannot be taken back. Esau was so mad that he wanted to kill his brother! But their mother, Rebecca, helped Jacob escape to a far land. It wasn't until twenty years later that the brothers reunited and could offer forgiveness to one another.

STEP BY STEP

Forgiveness is not a quick process. The bigger the mountain, the longer it takes to climb it. And the bigger the hurt, the longer it can take to complete the journey of forgiveness.

Even though forgiveness takes us a long time to figure out, Jesus sticks with us. He knows how hard it is to forgive. Psalm 80 describes how we can respond when God restores us. Circle the word "restore" in the following passage.

> **"Then we will not turn away from you; revive us, and we will call on your name. Restore us, Lord God Almighty; make your face shine on us, that we may be saved." Psalm 80:18-19**

The first move in restoration is always God's. When God restores us, we are able to call on God's name. We can thank Him and turn to Him.

Because of His love, we don't have to lose hope, even in the worst of tragedies. When that pear tree was cut down to a stump, it rose up from the ashes of 9/11, thanks to the tender care of the plant doctors. We too can rise up, with the tender care of God, our Great Physician. We too can rise from the ashes.

CHALLENGE

It took nine years for the pear tree to be restored.

How old will you be in nine years? _____

It took twenty years before Jacob and Esau were reunited.

How old will you be in twenty years? _____

#FORGIVINGCHALLENGEKIDS

It's hard to imagine waiting years to receive complete forgiveness. Is there something that happened a long time ago that you need to forgive or apologize for? If so, write it on the calendar below. Make a plan to talk to someone about that hurt or to apologize once and for all. Make a plan to rise up and fix that hurt.

If nothing comes to mind, copy Psalm 80:18-19 into your calendar below. Use it as your prayer of thanks to God for His forgiveness of your sin.

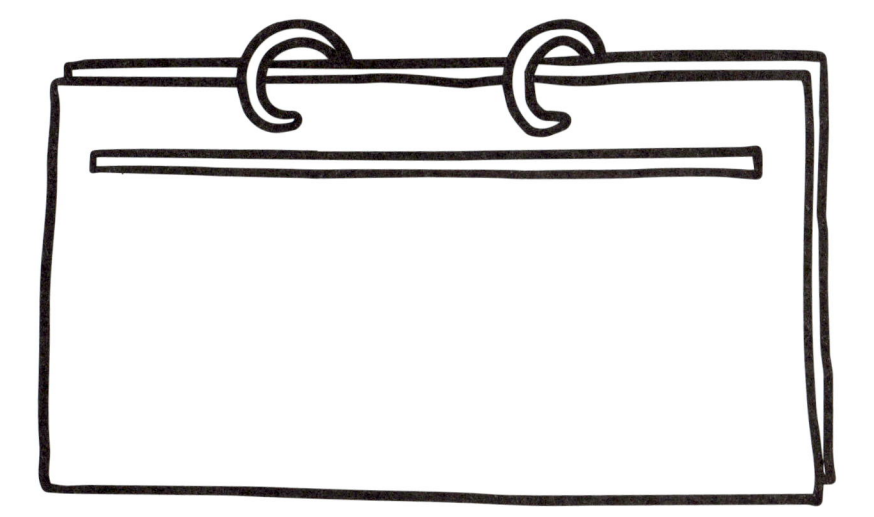

RED ALERT!

Jacob and Esau, twin sons of Isaac and Rebekah, even fought in the womb! And when they were born, Jacob was clutching on to Esau's heel (Genesis 25:21-26). So Jacob pestered Esau from the very beginning.

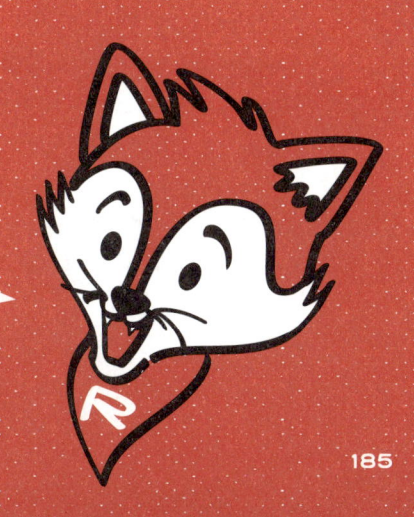

DAY 29
THE RISE-UP: RESTORATION
BUT I'M STILL MAD!

ZIGGING AND ZAGGING

On a journey up a mountain, you will never travel in a straight line. In fact, many mountains have trails called "switchbacks." A switchback is a path that zig-zags back and forth up a mountain.

Switchbacks are useful for many reasons:

- They keep the path from becoming too steep.
- They keep the soil and rocks from getting loose and hitting others below or making hikers slip.
- They keep the trail from excessive erosion when rain falls. (Erosion is when soil is moved from one place to another, by water or wind.)

There are many switchbacks along the road to forgiveness.

EMOTIONAL SWITCHBACKS

Even after you forgive someone, you may still have lingering feelings of anger. Memories of what happened might stir up this anger.

Trying to forgive without dealing with these feelings is like trying to climb straight up the mountain. The path is steeper and very difficult, and you'll have some exhausting back sliding.

Remember the story from Day 10, when Corrie ten Boom told the miracle of how she forgave the German guard at the death camp? After learning to forgive a murderous guard, you'd think that forgiving her friends for the minor things they did would be a piece of cake. Right?

Wrong. Corrie says she still felt angry at her friends, and she still had to keep going back to God, asking Him to give her the strength to forgive. As she put it, "I was (restored) to my Father."

The path of forgiveness is not a straight line. It zigs and zags, like switchbacks. One day we'll feel calm and forgiveness comes easily. But on another day, we'll feel angry, and forgiveness is tough. Maybe it will feel like you cannot ever trust the other person again.

Our emotions can make us feel like we are on switchbacks.

- They often make the journey longer.
- They make you feel like your moods are all over the place, instead of making progress in the relationship.
- You may feel like you keep having the same conversations over and over again.

Even though it can feel long and hard, it's important to not give up. When hurt and anger seem to slow your progress, look to the Bible to see the best way to wrestle with our emotions.

DEALINGS WITH FEELINGS

There are two ways that people will tell you to deal with your feelings.

1. Stuff everything inside and ignore your feelings.
2. Let your feelings be your guide. Pour out all your feelings and never apologize for them.

The Bible has a third way to deal with our feelings. King David writes in the Psalms, **"Give your burdens to the Lord, and he will take care of you. He will not permit the godly to slip and fall." Psalm 55:22 (NLT)**

Feelings aren't bad, but they shouldn't control us. When you feel strong emotions come over you, take them to God.

Peter, one of Jesus's disciples, writes a similar message for us. He says, **"Give all your worries and cares to God, for he cares about you." 1 Peter 5:7 (NLT)**

God isn't angry at you for having feelings and emotions when you're trying to forgive. But He also doesn't want you to be a slave to your emotions. So turn to Him and ask for His help in controlling your anger or sadness.

Jesus understands your feelings and emotions because He was true God and true man. Only because He was true God and true man at the same time was Jesus able to forgive all sin. Because He died and rose again, we are able to rise up and work through our emotions.

#FORGIVINGCHALLENGEKIDS

CHALLENGE

Write about your own journey of forgiveness on the picture of the mountain below. If you don't have a personal story of forgiveness, then make up a scenario. At the bottom of the mountain, write down what happened. Then, at each switchback, write down a feeling or emotion that you had on the journey of forgiveness. (You can choose from the list below or use your own.)

Repeat 1 Peter 5:7 at each switchback. Give those emotions to God.

EMOTIONS

Sadness	Excitement	Confusion	Guilt
Joy	Awkwardness	Hope	Hatred
Anger	Anxiety	Shame	Love
Fear	Awe	Annoyance	Frustration

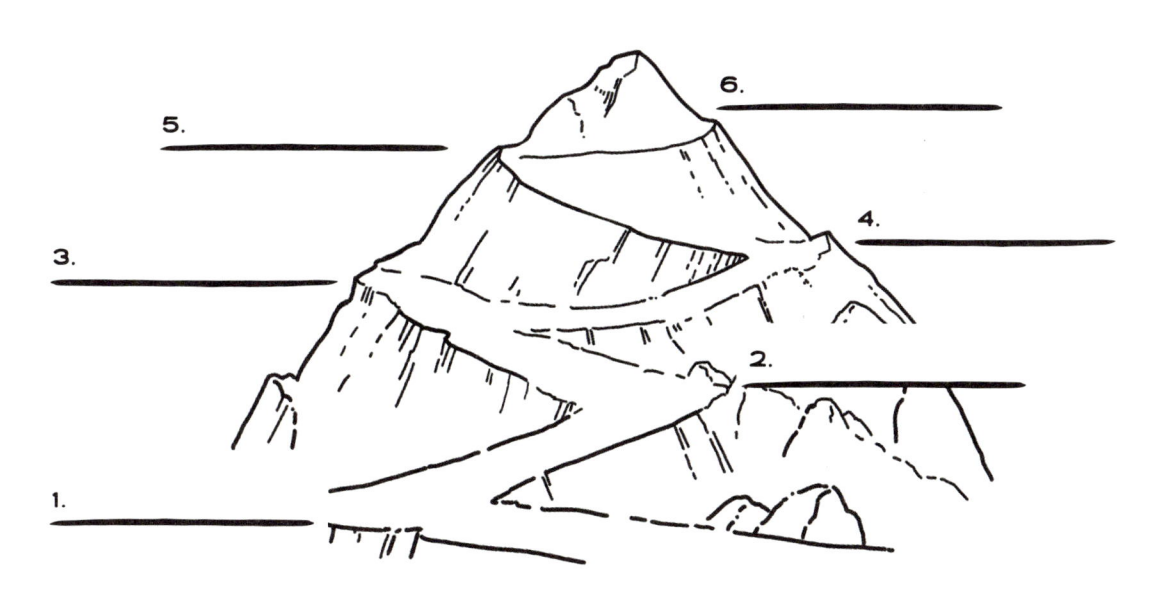

WHAT HAPPENED: _____

THE RISE-UP • 189

DAY 30
THE RISE-UP RESTORATION
FORGIVENESS HAPPENS IN THE DARK

RISING THROUGH THE DARKNESS

Mrs. Thompson, Parker's second-grade teacher, didn't like him. She didn't call on him in class, she ignored the gifts he brought, and she rarely gave him much attention. It wasn't that she was ever mean to him. She simply ignored him most of the time.

Parker thought he must have done something wrong to deserve her icy treatment. But as Parker grew older and had other teachers, he realized how unfairly she had treated him. He was not a bad student and did not misbehave in class. Parker had good manners and got along with other kids.

It took a long time for him to trust teachers again. Parker tried to imagine what would have caused Mrs. Thompson to act the way she did. Maybe she was going through a tough time with her family, or she was sick and didn't tell anyone. Perhaps she had some secret stress in her life and took it out on him. Maybe he reminded her of someone who had hurt her in the past.

But no matter how many excuses Parker thought of, he didn't see how she could be so cruel.

IN THE DARK

People often use the phrase "I'm in the dark" to describe how it feels to not understand something. That's how Parker felt about Mrs. Thompson. He was "in the dark" about why she was not kind. In our journey of rising up, there will be times when we will not understand why someone hurt us. It may feel like we are in a pitch black hole or like a seed stuck under the ground.

For a seed to grow, it must first be separated from the plant and fall to the ground. After it is buried, something new will begin to grow out of it. Jesus talks about this right before He died.

> **"Very truly I tell you, unless a kernel of wheat falls to the ground and dies, it remains only a single seed. But if it dies, it produces many seeds."**
> **John 12:24**

As Jesus says, a grain of wheat cannot produce many seeds until it is buried and dies. The grain of wheat is "in the dark." If a wheat grain could think, it might be wondering why it had to die and fall to the ground.

In the same way, some things will happen to us that we simply cannot make sense of. We have to do our forgiveness "in the dark," not knowing why something happened.

WHAT DID I DO TO DESERVE THIS?

WHY ME?

TRUST HIM

Right before Jesus talked about the kernel of wheat falling to the ground, this is what He said: **"The hour has come for the Son of Man to be glorified." John 12:23**

Jesus knew He would be nailed to the cross very soon. When He said that a kernel had to fall and die, He was talking about His own death. But instead of thinking that this was the end, Jesus described it as a time that He would be glorified. Can you believe it? The disciples could not make any sense out of what He was saying.

Even though no one at that time believed that Jesus's death was their saving grace, He died anyway.

- He died for all the times you won't understand.
- He died for all who were hurt unfairly.
- He even died for those who are mean for no good reason.

Finally, Jesus warned us that we all will experience a death or darkness of some sort. He said, **"Anyone who loves their life will lose it, while anyone who hates their life in this world will keep it for eternal life." John 12:25**

Jesus doesn't want you to hate your life or stay buried deep in the dark. Jesus wants you to trust Him to never leave you, even when things look dark. When you feel like you are sinking down in confusion, have hope that Jesus will never leave you alone in the dark.

He is the Light.

#FORGIVINGCHALLENGEKIDS

CHALLENGE

Plant a seed. Keep it in a place where it can get plenty of sunshine and water. As you plant that seed, think about an area of unforgiveness in your life. Imagine what that seed might look like under the ground. As you wait and watch, don't give up hope that the seed will sprout.

Imagine what it would feel like for that little shoot to come poking through the ground. One day, like that seed, you too will rise and have a new life in Jesus. Trust that God will answer prayer and bring forgiveness in your life.

RED ALERT!

The day that Jesus was crucified was the darkest day in history. The Gospels say that a darkness fell over the land from the sixth hour (noon) to the ninth hour (3 p.m.). Matthew 27:46 says: Jesus then "cried out in a loud voice, *'Eli, Eli, lema sabachthani?'* (which means *'My God, my God, why have you forsaken me?'*)."
Three days later, He rose again.

DAY 31
THE RISE-UP: RESTORATION
FORGIVENESS COMES FIRST

THE WIZARD OF OZ

If you have a nickname, write it here: _____

If not, come up with a catchy nickname for yourself: _____

Nicknames are given for many reasons, but they're often based on something you did or said. For example, baseball player Ozzie Smith was nicknamed "The Wizard of Oz" because he made such spectacular catches and plays. Sometimes, his nickname was shortened to "The Wizard" or "Oz."

Oz was also known for beginning every opening day by doing a backflip while walking out to his position. Talk about a trick play! He went on to be a 15-time All-Star, 13-time Gold Glove winner, and a 1982 World Series champion with the St. Louis Cardinals.

Ozzie was given his nickname because of what he did on the field. But Jesus gave His disciple Peter a new name, even BEFORE he did anything to deserve the name.

THE ROCK

Before he met Jesus, Peter's name was Simon son of Jonah. Simon means "hear" or "listen." But Jesus changed Simon's name to "Peter," which means "rock." It was not until years later that Peter showed why he was called "rock." Check out this passage from the Book of Matthew:

> "When Jesus came to the region of Caesarea Philippi, he asked his disciples, 'Who do people say the Son of Man is?'
>
> "They replied, 'Some say John the Baptist; others say Elijah; and still others, Jeremiah or one of the prophets.'
>
> "'But what about you?' he asked. 'Who do you say I am?'
>
> "Simon Peter answered, 'You are the Messiah, the Son of the living God.'
>
> "Jesus replied, 'Blessed are you, Simon son of Jonah, for this was not revealed to you by flesh and blood, but by my Father in heaven. And I tell you that you are Peter, and on this rock I will build my church, and the gates of Hades will not overcome it.'" Matthew 16:13-18

In this passage, the other disciples weren't exactly sure who Jesus really was. They answered Jesus's question by saying people thought He was John the Baptist or Elijah or Jeremiah. Only Peter blurted out the truth: "You are the Messiah, the Son of the living God."

Peter knew the truth and spoke the truth. He was a rock. But following Jesus and getting a new name did not mean that Peter changed overnight. He had plenty of mess-ups, such as when he denied knowing Jesus after His Lord had been arrested. But after the resurrection, Peter showed how incredibly brave he could be, preaching about Jesus even though it put his life in danger.

FORGIVEN PEOPLE FORGIVE

Like Peter, you will not change immediately. Walking along the journey of forgiveness does not mean your feelings are changed overnight. It takes many little steps, one at a time.

The point is…Peter didn't have to earn his new name—"the Rock." The name came first, and then he showed courage. It's the same with forgiveness. We don't have to earn it. We receive forgiveness from God first. Then this enables us to become more forgiving people. Forgiven people forgive.

Walking along the journey of forgiveness does not mean your feelings are changed overnight. It takes many little steps, one at a time. But knowing who you are in Christ is the first step to growing into who He called you to be. So what name has Jesus given to you?

RED ALERT!

> Jesus's name was very common and ordinary. It was the "John Smith" of the first century. But that doesn't mean it was meaningless. The name "Jesus" means "Yahweh saves."

He calls you His child, His most treasured possession. He gives you this name, even BEFORE you do anything to deserve it. That's because you don't need to live up to your new name to be included in God's family. You're already in. Now that's a reason to do a backflip!

CHALLENGE

Jesus calls you many wonderful names in the Bible. Here are only a few:

- Child of God (John 1:12)
- Redeemed (Ephesians 1:7)
- Forgiven (Ephesians 1:7)
- God's Handiwork (Ephesians 2:10)
- Image of God (Genesis 1:27)
- Conquerors (Romans 8:37)
- Friend of God (John 15:15)
- Citizen of Heaven (Philippians 3:20)
- Fruit Bearers (John 15:16)
- Holy Nation (1 Peter 2:9)
- Royal Priesthood (1 Peter 2:9)
- Special Possession (1 Peter 2:9)

Pick one of the names that God has given you and fill out the sentence below. As a bonus, listen to the song "Who You Say I Am" by Hillsong.

"I am _____ (your name).

Because I am (a) _____ (Bible nickname),

I can forgive others who hurt me."

DAY 32
THE RISE-UP: RESTORATION
FORGIVING YOURSELF

LOVE YOUR NEIGHBOR AS YOURSELF

In a survey conducted by Pastor Zach Zehnder for the book *Forgiving Challenge*, most of the adults responded that it was harder to forgive themselves than to forgive someone else.

To forgive someone, it usually means the person has done something to hurt you. So, to forgive *yourself*, you have to ask: "Can you hurt yourself?"

You bet you can! In fact, you probably will be the person who is most hurt by your mistakes. So, if you can hurt yourself, can you also forgive yourself?

The Bible never says the words "forgive yourself," so some people think we don't even need to worry about it. But Jesus does say that we should love ourselves. He said in Matthew 22:39b, **"Love your neighbor as yourself."**

Note that it says "as yourself." That means you love your neighbor AND you love yourself. But loving yourself has a limit. The Bible says that loving yourself can go too far if it becomes selfishness, and Timothy groups it with a lot of other negative things. **"For people will be lovers of self, lovers of money, proud, arrogant, abusive, disobedient to their parents, ungrateful, unholy."**
2 Timothy 3:2 (ESV)

Another way to look at it is we can love ourselves only as much as we love other people. This applies to forgiveness as well. We can forgive others only as much as we have accepted God's forgiveness.

So, you might say that in addition to "loving our neighbor as yourself," we should "forgive our neighbor as we are forgiven by God."

WALKING THE TIGHTROPE

Pastor Timothy Keller says, "We are more sinful and flawed in ourselves than we ever dared to believe, yet at the very same time we are more loved and accepted in Jesus Christ than we ever dared hope."

But does loving and forgiving yourself mean that what you do is okay? Not at all. If you believe everything you do is okay, then that means you do not think you really need God. You're saving yourself through your "not so bad-ness."

On the other hand, if you hate yourself and can't accept the forgiveness God offers, you're making yourself bigger than God. You're deciding what God can and can't forgive.

As Keller says, being a Christian is the perfect tightrope. The Christian life means not thinking TOO MUCH of yourself and not thinking TOO LITTLE of yourself. God reveals your sin through the Ten Commandments. (Look back at Day 13 to review the Ten Commandments.) But God is also revealed through Jesus our Savior, who keeps you from thinking too low of yourself. Look back at Day 31 for all the wonderful names God calls you.

You are restored back into a good relationship with Jesus, no matter what you have done. Jesus has chosen not to hold your sins against you. **"For I will forgive**

their iniquity, and I will remember their sin no more" Jeremiah 31:34b (ESV)

In other words, when you become a Christian, you're fully embraced by God's grace. **"Therefore, there is now no condemnation for those who are in Christ Jesus,"** says Romans 8:1.

Because of Jesus, no one can accuse you or condemn you anymore.

Not even yourself!

CHALLENGE

Complete this forgiveness letter from God.

Dear _____ (your name),

I'm here. If you need a good cry, I will be right here with you. I know you are feeling bad about _____
(an action you are having a hard time feeling forgiven for).
I was there when it happened. I didn't leave you then, and I won't leave you now. There is nothing you can ever do to lose my love. I will protect you until you die, and even after that I will have a perfect place for you. I can fix the mess-ups you have made. I am stronger than
_____ (a sin in your life) and I am braver than
_____ (an enemy in your life). Nothing can exhaust me.
I love you,
God

#FORGIVINGCHALLENGEKIDS

RED ALERT!

> Paul the apostle wrote 13 letters in the New Testament, and the Letter to the Romans is the longest. Martin Luther, the leader of the Reformation, was studying Romans when he discovered that the Bible was teaching that we are saved by faith alone, not by our good works.

#FORGIVINGCHALLENGEKIDS

DAY 33

THE RISE-UP: RESTORATION
GOD'S PLAN TO RESTORE THE WORLD

OUR BROKEN WORLD

So far, we've learned how we can rise up above our feelings, restore broken relationships, and even forgive ourselves. But God also has big plans to restore the world as well.

International Mountain Day on December 11 is a reminder to organizations and communities to help mountain people protect the land they live in, improve their livelihoods, and keep mountain environments healthy. Caring for our world, including the mountains, is one way that we can honor God.

As we learned on Day 6, God put Adam and Eve in the Garden of Eden and told them to care for and nurture the land. That job continues to this day. We are called to take care of the world that God made. But when we look around, we see that it is not always happening.

- There is pollution in our beautiful oceans and lakes.
- Disease spreads because people don't have warm homes and healthy food to eat.
- The glaciers melt and rain forests are cut down.

The world isn't just broken on the outside. People and relationships are also broken.

- Families break apart in divorce.
- War tears countries apart.
- Poverty and greed divides people.

It breaks God's heart to see pain in the world. When sin entered the world, things began to crumble quickly. But even after God watched His perfect creation fall apart, He had a plan to restore the Earth back to what it was.

THE GREAT RESCUE PLAN

When Adam and Eve sinned, we call that "The Fall." In her book, *The Epic of Eden*, Sandra L. Richter compares the fall of Adam to a mountain climber who has fallen from a great height.

"Adam now lies broken and bloody on the ledge of a cliff—too far from top or bottom for a simple rescue," Richter says. "It will take a series of rescues to bring this climber to safety."

As she notes, somebody will have to "rappel" (climb down with ropes) to reach the injured climber. That person will have to give the injured climber first aid and then strap him to a stretcher. After the climber is hoisted back to the top of the mountain, a helicopter may need to fly him to a hospital. Then doctors need to work tirelessly to save his life. Finally, the climber may have to spend time in an intensive care unit.

So you see, his rescue is a series of *many steps*. Richter says God's rescue of the world is like that. It's been a series of steps. There was Noah, then Abraham, then

Moses and David. All of these were steps in God's rescue plan. But Jesus was the most important step of all. Through Him, sin was conquered.

THY KINGDOM COME

Could God have just scrapped everything and started over when Adam and Eve sinned? Yes. But that is not God's character. He doesn't just give up on the world, and He won't give up on His people. In the last book of the Bible, John has a vision of Heaven:

> **"Then the angel showed me the river of the water of life, as clear as crystal, flowing from the throne of God and of the Lamb down the middle of the great street of the city. On each side of the river stood the tree of life, bearing twelve crops of fruit, yielding its fruit every month. And the leaves of the tree are for the healing of the nations. No longer will there be any curse. The throne of God and of the Lamb will be in the city, and his servants will serve him." Revelation 22:1-3**

God's plan is to rescue and restore the world back to the way it used to be in Eden, and we get to be a part of that. This plan is already in effect.

When Jesus was on earth, He talked a lot about the Kingdom of Heaven. The Kingdom of Heaven is anywhere that God has ultimate control. Because you have Jesus in your heart, you are part of the Kingdom right now. And when you work to clean up the world and fix relationships, you're helping to bring the Kingdom of God to earth. We even pray it in the Lord's Prayer when we say, "Thy Kingdom come."

God is the only one who can completely restore this world, but He has given you a chance to be a part of His redemption plan.

#FORGIVINGCHALLENGEKIDS

CHALLENGE

Do a neighborhood clean-up or trash pick-up at a local park. Even if it's just your own street, see how you can help be a part of redeeming this world. Forgiveness isn't just about wiping away sin. It's also about bringing things back into a good relationship.

RED ALERT!

The vision in Revelation of the river of life doesn't just remind us of Eden. It also recalls Ezekiel's vision of a river flowing from the Temple to the Dead Sea (Ezekiel 47:1-12). The Dead Sea is called "dead" because it has so much salt in it that few forms of life (except microorganisms) can survive. But God brings life to dead places. Even Dead Seas.

DAYS 34-40
OF THE 40-DAY CHALLENGE

THE STEP-UP:
SANCTIF

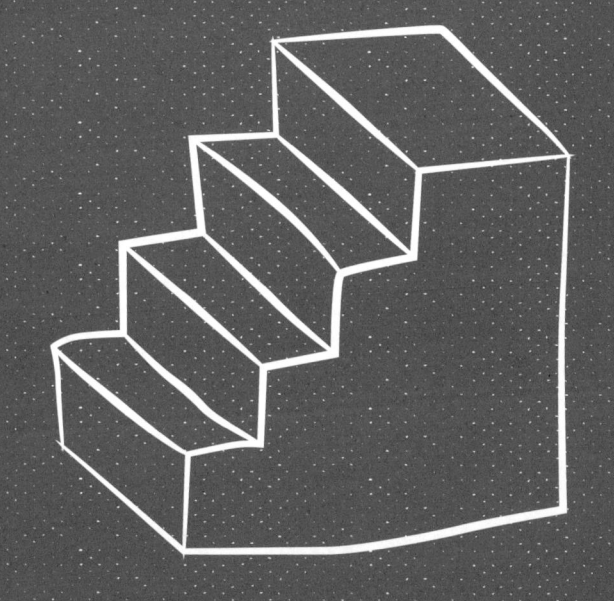

ICATION

HAVE FUN COLORING THIS PAGE!
FIND MORE LIKE THIS AT FORGIVINGCHALLENGE.COM/KIDS

THE MOUNTAINS OF REDVALE

PART 6

Isabella watched in horror as her brother and Frankie tumbled into the heart of the volcano.

Why did we ever have to come to Redvale again? she thought. *Danger is everywhere, so something like this was bound to happen eventually! What are we going to tell our parents? "Sorry, Mom and Dad, Aiden fell into a volcano."*

To make matters worse, they heard a growing rumble from below.

"Off of the bridge!" Malachi shouted. "Get off now!"

No sooner did they scurry off of the bridge and climb into a cave than a big burst of green slime came roaring up from the depths of the volcano. From inside the cave, they saw a geyser of slime come shooting upward—up, up, up to the peak of the volcano.

Where was Aiden in all of this? Isabella wondered. *Had he just been slimed?*

ERUPTION!

Yes, Aiden had just been slimed. And so had Frankie. As the two boys tumbled toward the bottom of the volcano, Aiden could only think about how stupid he had been. Why did he have to fight Frankie on a narrow bridge? What was he thinking?

But then he noticed something green rising upward in the volcano as they plunged downward. Slime! The volcano was belching once again, and a massive column of slime was shooting up, coming straight at them.

Slamming into squishy slime turned out to be much better than landing on rock at the bottom of a volcano. The slime geyser hit them head-on and carried the two boys skyward. It was like being carried up by a fountain of green goo. It was sticky and smelly, but at least they were still alive.

By this time, Aiden had lost sight of Frankie. All he could see were waves of slime on all sides, lifting him higher and higher. Was the volcano erupting? If so, the slime would only delay their destruction. Once they were spouted from the top of the volcano, surely they would come crashing down to the ground. That would be the end of them.

Carried by the slime, they burst into the light, shooting from the top of the volcano at tremendous speed. As he tumbled all around, Aiden couldn't tell if he was upside down or right side up. He caught sight of Frankie a couple of times, and he too was flipping around, completely out of control.

When fountains spit up water, the water eventually falls back to earth. That's what happened here. The slime spit them up into the air and then fell back toward the ground. So did Aiden and Frankie.

Falling, Aiden looked straight down and saw the ground coming toward him extremely fast. He braced himself for a bone-breaking crash as they rocketed down with Superman speed.

But as these images flickered through his mind, Aiden saw movement off to his right. Something large was racing up the side of the volcano, churning up stones and soil. Was that what he thought it was?

This large "something" reached the top of the volcano just in time to hurl itself out of the ground. It was Bob the Cave Whale! Aiden couldn't believe how high Bob could heave himself into the air. Bob's enormous mouth was wide open, and he was coming straight for Aiden and Frankie. Aiden prayed that the whale timed his leap right.

Bob the Cave Whale snagged the two boys in mid-air, like a dog snagging a Frisbee, and his mouth clamped down with a crunching crash. Now they were in complete darkness, sliding down slippery rock, feeling a sudden blast of cool air. With a splash, they finally came to a stop in a puddle in Bob's stomach.

#FORGIVINGCHALLENGEKIDS

Aiden spotted Frankie moving around, just a few feet to his right. Frankie was on his back, thrashing in the water and rising into a sitting position.

"Where in the world are we?" Frankie asked, crawling over to Aiden.

"You wouldn't believe me if I told you," Aiden said.

"Try me."

"We're in the belly of a whale."

"You're right. I don't believe you."

SWORDS IN THE STONE

Suddenly, all was calm inside the volcano. The eruption was over, and green slime was no longer shooting up from the bottom of the mountain. Emily and the others were huddled in a cave, where they heard the distant sound of falling rocks. But other than that, all was quiet.

"Is it safe to step out of the cave?" Emily asked.

"It is," said Malachi, motioning everyone forward, back onto the bridge. "No time to lose. We have to cross the bridge before the next eruption."

"Cross the bridge?" Chloe exclaimed. "And how are we going to do that? There's a huge chunk of it missing!"

Emily wondered the same thing. There was about a six-foot gap in the stone bridge, where it had collapsed beneath Aiden and Frankie's feet. No way could they jump across that space!

"Red, you know what to do, don't you?" Malachi asked, looking down on the little fox.

"Absolutely! First…the sword." Red reached into Balthazar's saddlebag and drew out the first of the two golden swords—the swords that had been used to slice through the spider webs.

"What use is a sword in getting across this bridge?" Emily asked.

"Watch and learn," Red said. "I'm the only one here who can jump that far."

With his sword held high, Red got a good running start and then sailed across the gap in the bridge. It's amazing how high and far a fox could leap. It's like he had springs in his legs. Red skidded when he landed on the other side, but he made it. Then, raising the golden sword high with his two paws, he drove the blade deep into the stone.

"I still don't get it," said Chloe. "What's a sword in the stone going to do to help us?"

"Watch and learn," said Malachi. On their side of the broken bridge, Malachi held up the second golden sword and drove its blade deep into the rock. Now, there was a sword anchored on both sides of the broken bridge.

Next, Malachi tied a rope to the base of the first sword, and he hurled the other end to Red. The fox tied his end of the rope to the second sword. They did the same with two other lengths of rope, until there were three slender strands strung across the gap, from one sword to the other.

"You want us to climb across the gap on those ropes?" Chloe said.

"No," said Balthazar. "That's much too dangerous. I want you to climb across ME."

"What are you talking about?"

"Are you sure you want to do this, Balthazar?" asked Malachi.

"It's the only way," said the donkey. "Greater love has no one than this: to lay down one's life for one's friends."

With those words, Balthazar climbed out on the three strands of rope and lay belly-down across them.

"Hurry," said Malachi, tying another rope around Emily's waist. "Crawl across Balthazar's body, while there is still time."

"You want me to cross Balthazar?"

"If you fall, I've got you with this rope."

"But what about Balthazar?"

"I'll be fine," said the donkey. "Just hurry before the volcano erupts again."

Emily did as he asked. She got on her hands and knees and slowly began to crawl across Balthazar's back. The donkey swayed under her weight, but he remained balanced on the three ropes.

#FORGIVINGCHALLENGEKIDS

"I'm so sorry," Emily said, as she reached his neck. "I hope I'm not hurting you."

"Nothing to be sorry about. You're as light as a feather."

As Emily crawled up Balthazar's neck, she whispered into one of his big, floppy ears: "Thank you for doing this. I love you, Balthazar."

"And I love you, little one."

DOC ROCK

Back inside the belly of the whale, Aiden tried to explain everything to Frankie. "Bob is our friend."

"Bob?" Frankie said. "Who's Bob?"

"He's the Cave Whale, and we're inside his belly."

"Cave Whale? What's a Cave Whale?"

"It's a cave that looks just like a whale and swims beneath the surface of the ground. Bob the Cave Whale just saved us."

"And just in the nick of time," said one of the rocks behind them. Frankie nearly jumped out of his shoes in shock.

"What in the world! Did that rock just talk to us?"

"I sure did," said Rockette. "You're new to Redvale, aren't you? My name is Rockette Boulder, the daughter of Orville Boulder, son of Homer Boulder, son of Mookie Boulder, son of Leo Boulder, son of…"

Rockette rattled off names for the next two minutes before Aiden finally said, "Okay, okay, we get the picture. We're immensely grateful to Bob for saving us. But can he let us out of his belly now?"

"No can do," said Rockette.

"What do you mean he can't let us out?" Aiden knocked on the walls of the cave and shouted, "Hey Bob, if you can hear me, LET US GO FREE!"

"Save your breath," said Rockette. "He's not going to let you out until you've seen a doctor."

Aiden studied his arms and legs. "Why do I need a doctor? I'm not hurt. See? Frankie, are you hurt?"

Frankie looked down at his legs and said, "I seem to be fine too. It's a miracle, but I'm okay."

"Maybe you're all right on the outside. It's your insides I'm worried about," said Rockette. The boulder swiveled around and shouted into the darkness. "Doc! Hey doc, are you back there?"

"Hold your horses," came a voice from the darkness. "And hold your donkeys and giraffes too." Then a small light flicked on, and a moving stack of rocks glided into view. The Doc kind of looked like a snowman, but instead of balls of snow piled on top of one another, this creature was made out of various boulders, piled on top of one another. The top rock had two eyes and a mouth. He also had a light positioned on his forehead, held in place by a strap.

"Let me introduce you to Doc Rock," said Rockette. "He's going to give you an exam."

"I hate tests," said Frankie.

"Not a school exam," said Doc Rock. "I'm giving you an inside-out exam. Stick out your tongue and say, 'Ahhhhh.'"

Before Aiden knew what was happening, Doc Rock was sticking a wooden tongue depressor in his mouth—like a regular human doctor.

"Say, 'Ahhhhh,'" Doc commanded.

"Ahhhhh," Aiden responded, as the doctor peered inside his mouth.

"Hmmmm," the doctor said. "Just as I thought." Then he swung around to face Frankie and snapped, "Open up and say 'Ahhhhh.'"

Frankie looked over at Aiden, who just shrugged. "The sooner you do as he says, the sooner we'll get out of here."

So Frankie opened wide, and Doc Rock peered inside, muttering to himself the entire time. Finally, he pulled back and said, "Just as I suspected."

"What's wrong?" Aiden asked.

"Both of you are suffering from Trash Rash," he said. "One of the worst cases I've seen."

#FORGIVINGCHALLENGEKIDS

"What in the world is he talking about?" Frankie said to Aiden. "And why are we even listening to a pile of rocks?"

Doc Rock glared at Frankie. "I'll have you know that this pile of rocks has been practicing inside-out medicine for twenty years! And I know a case of Trash Rash when I see it!"

"And what is Trash Rash?" Aiden asked, trying to calm things down.

"Some call it Trash Tongue or Rash Tongue, but I prefer Trash Rash because it rhymes. It's when you constantly use your tongue to trash-talk about other people or brag about yourself. You two do a lot of both, but especially the bragging part. And until you can control your tongues, you're going to have a hard time truly forgiving each other."

"I'd listen to him," said Rockette. "He cured me of Trash Rash two years ago."

"The Bible says, 'The tongue is a small part of the body, but it makes great boasts,'" Doc Rock said. "It also said that out of the same mouth comes praise and cursing."

"It's just like this volcano," Rockette added. "Praise and cursing come from our mouths, and both pure water and green slime comes out of these mountains. Which one do you prefer?"

"Pure water?" Frankie said, as if he wasn't sure of the right answer.

"But Trash Rash is not your only problem," said Doc Rock, gliding behind Aiden. "You've also got a bad case of the Grudges."

"The what?"

Aiden felt Doc Rock grab at something on his back. Then the doctor gave a mighty yank, and Aiden felt a sensation like ripping a bandage off quickly. Doc Rock glided in front of him, holding a strange brown creature with suction cups for legs. It was about the size of a shoe, and it had two beady eyes.

"You've been holding on to this Grudge for a year now," Doc Rock said, tossing the creature into the darkness. It went scurrying away, squeaking. "But I'm not done."

Doc Rock slipped behind Aiden and pulled off three more Grudges. Then he did the same with Frankie, yanking eight Grudges from his back.

"Ow!! How come I never saw those before?" Frankie said. "I didn't even know they were there."

"That's the way with Grudges. You're often not even aware that you're holding a Grudge—or that they're holding on to you. Grudges will whisper in your ear, and you don't even know it."

"Whisper in our ears?" Aiden said. "What about?"

"A Grudge stores up bad feelings that you have for other people. And it whispers those bad feelings in your ears. Take you two, for example. Most of those Grudges were whispering bad feelings about each of you."

Aiden and Frankie exchanged glances. "But we made peace with each other," Aiden said.

"Not completely," said Doc Rock, pulling out a notepad and scribbling. "Being a peacemaker is something you have to do all the time, like taking medicines and vitamins on a daily basis. Speaking of which…"

Doc Rock ripped off one piece of paper and handed it to Aiden. Then he ripped a second page from his notepad and handed it to Frankie.

"Those are my prescriptions for you both," he said. "Do this five times a day, and I think your Grudges will be gone for good."

Aiden looked down at his paper and read these words: "Speak the truth in love. You will grow to become in every respect the mature body of him who is the head, that is, Christ."

"Speak the truth in love," Doc Rock said. "That's the cure. You need BOTH truth and love."

Aiden and Frankie looked up from their slips of paper and stared at one another. Aiden knew what he should say, but was it difficult. To his amazement, Frankie spoke first.

"He's right, Aiden. I apologize for all of the mean things I said to you."

#FORGIVINGCHALLENGEKIDS

"And to others," Doc Rock was quick to point out. "You also said mean things about him to his classmates."

"Right. You're right."

Aiden wished he had been the first to speak up, but Frankie was always beating him at things. Frankie was better at baseball and soccer, which made Aiden really mad. And now Frankie had been the first to apologize. He was always first!

"And don't worry that Frankie was first to say he's sorry," Doc Rock said, as if he knew exactly what Aiden was thinking. "I know you like to make everything a contest, but this isn't a game, Aiden."

"You're right, Doc. And you're right as well, Frankie. I'm sorry for being mad at you for being better than me in baseball and soccer."

"Really? I was always mad at you because I thought you were better than me!" Frankie said with a growing grin. "That's why I played dirty in our games. I thought it was the only way I could win against you."

"You know, you two are very much alike," said Rockette. "You could almost be brothers."

"We are brothers," said Frankie, sticking out his hand. Smiling broadly, Aiden reached out and shook it.

At that very moment, the inside of Bob the Cave Whale began to shake.

"Well, I think my work here is done," said Doc Rock, gliding off into the darkness.

"Hang on!" shouted Rockette. "Get ready for a big belch."

Bob the Cave Whale let loose with the loudest belch Aiden had ever heard, and a blast of air struck them from behind, sending them flying forward.

"WHOOOOOAH!"

Aiden and Frankie flew out of Bob's mouth and landed hard on the ground. When Aiden looked up, he found himself on the side of Mount Goel. But even more importantly, the grinning faces of Malachi, Red, Isabella, Chloe, and Balthazar were staring back at him.

BRIDGE-BUILDERS

"You're alive!" Emily shouted, as she and Isabella ran forward to give Aiden a hug. "And you're wet!" she also said, pulling back.

"How did you guys get out of the volcano alive?" Aiden asked. "It erupted!"

"We worked together," Balthazar said.

"Balthazar is being too modest," said Red, bounding up beside the donkey. "Balthazar saved us! He turned his body into a bridge!"

Emily didn't know that donkeys could blush. But Balthazar was definitely blushing.

"We are all asked to be a bridge to one another," the donkey said.

"I don't get it," said Frankie.

"A bridge takes you from one side to the other," Malachi said. "When you make friends, when you're a peacemaker, you're building a bridge between people. But Jesus is the ultimate bridge-builder. He created a bridge between us and God the Father. He laid down His life for us—just as Balthazar did."

"Remind me to get you a pizza when we return," Red said, patting the donkey's side.

"We're not out of danger yet," said Malachi. "I have a feeling that this mountain is not done erupting."

Malachi was exactly right. The mountain gave a sudden jolt, throwing everyone to the ground.

"Hurry, everyone!" shouted Bob the Cave Whale. "Everyone leap into my mouth! I'll protect you!"

But before anyone could even get back on their feet, let alone jump in Bob's mouth, the mountain blew its top. This eruption was a hundred times more fierce than the last one.

TO BE CONTINUED ON PAGE 256.

#FORGIVINGCHALLENGEKIDS

A Grudge stores up bad feelings that you have for other people. And it whispers those bad feelings in your ears.

#FORGIVINGCHALLENGEKIDS

DAY 34
THE STEP-UP: SANCTIFICATION
REDEMPTIVE REMEMBERING

WHAT IS SANCTIFICATION?

You have reached the final ascent—the final push up the mountain. So grab your oxygen and fasten your jackets! This may be the toughest week yet, but you can do it.

During this final week, we'll be studying the Step-up, or Sanctification. To "sanctify" something is to set it apart. If you are sanctified, that means you are different (in a good way), and we're going to study how forgiveness will make us different in this world. God uses forgiveness to set up His holy work, which we are invited to step upv into. You will learn about the new challenges that God has for you as a follower of Jesus.

Review the four phases of forgiveness so far by filling in the spaces next to the mountain below:

4. _____
3. _____
2. _____
1. _____

THE HIGHEST MOUNTAIN IN THE WORLD

People often say that the highest mountain in the world is Mount Everest. And if you measure it from sea level to the top, that is true. It is the highest at 29,029 feet. But if you included mountains that are partly underwater, a mountain in Hawaii has Everest beat.

Mauna Kea is 33,000 feet from its base to its peak, which is higher than Mount Everest. But a lot of it is covered by water. From sea level it is only 13,803 feet, which is much less than Everest.

In other words, when sizing up mountains, it matters where you start measuring. It also matters where you start when remembering hurts from your past. Ask yourself: Are you really seeing the full picture?

SEEING THE BIG PICTURE

In the Bible, Moses tells the Israelites to REMEMBER the hard times they went through. He reminds the people that they were caught in slavery, wandered in the wilderness, and had to flee from enemies.

- **SLAVERY**: "Remember that you were slaves in Egypt…" **Deuteronomy 15:15a**

- **WILDERNESS**: "Be careful that you do not forget the Lord your God…He led you through the vast and dreadful wilderness, that thirsty and waterless land, with its venomous snakes and scorpions." **Deuteronomy 8:11a and 15a**

- **ENEMIES**: "Remember what the Amalekites did to you along the way when you came out of Egypt. When you were weary and worn out, they met you on your journey and attacked all who were lagging behind; they had no fear of God." Deuteronomy 25:17-18

This may leave you scratching your head in confusion. Why in the world is Moses telling the Israelites to remember the bad times?

Moses encouraged the Israelites to remember painful situations to show them how God was working in their story all along. The pain was only part of the story—and only part of these verses.

Read the rest of the verses in bold type to see how each hard situation was redeemed.

- **SLAVERY**: "Remember that you were slaves in Egypt……**and the Lord your God redeemed you." Deuteronomy 15:15**

- **WILDERNESS**: **"For the Lord your God is bringing you into a good land—a land with brooks, streams, and deep springs gushing out into the valleys and hills…**…He led you through the vast and dreadful wilderness, that thirsty and waterless land, with its venomous snakes and scorpions." **Deuteronomy 8:7,15a**

- **ENEMIES**: "Remember what the Amalekites did to you along the way when you came out of Egypt. When you were weary and worn out, they met you on your journey and attacked all who were lagging behind; they had no fear of God……**When the Lord your God gives you rest from all the enemies around you in the land he is giving you to possess as an inheritance, you shall blot out the name of Amalek from under heaven. Do not forget!" Deuteronomy 25:17-19**

#FORGIVINGCHALLENGEKIDS

HEALED HURTS

The Israelites looked back at these memories from a safe place. They were invited to combine the really sad and hard memories with the moments that God was there for them. As a result, each hurt was combined with a heal. This is called Redemptive Remembering, or Healed Hurts.

- Instead of just remembering being in slavery, they combined it with the memory of being set free and redeemed.

- Instead of just remembering being in the wilderness, they thought about coming out of the desert and into the Promised Land.

- Instead of just remembering being attacked by an enemy, they also recalled rest and peace in their land and the promise that God will get revenge for their hurts.

ADJUST YOUR ZOOM

Think of our memories as a special kind of binoculars that make it possible for you to look back at the past. Sometimes our "memory binoculars" are zoomed in way too close when we look back at a hurt. We are so focused on the hurt that happened, we can't see anything that happened afterward.

Through God's grace and forgiveness, we can adjust our view and see more of what He sees. If we are forgiven, then we can look back at hard times and see how God was working. We can be healed people, not just hurt people. Jesus can redeem your past hurts. You will still remember those difficult times and painful moments, but you will see past failures as places where God invited you to step up and follow Him. With Jesus, our memory binoculars are set correctly.

CHALLENGE

Practice Redemptive Remembering. In the left lens of the binoculars below, write about a hurt you remember. How can Jesus help you zoom out to see this hurt more clearly? How did Jesus help you through the hurt? Answer that question in the second lens of the binoculars.

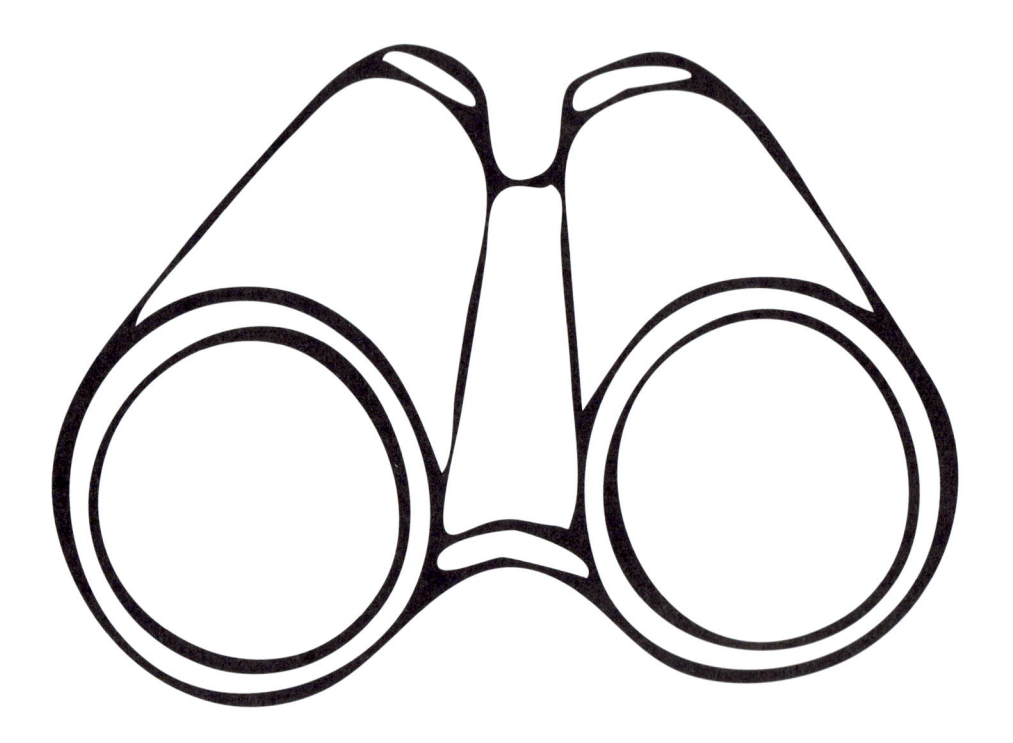

For fun, do some experiments with a camera today. Zoom in and take a picture of five objects around your house or classroom. But make sure the photo is super close-up. Then ask someone if they can identify the things pictured in the five close-up photos.

#FORGIVINGCHALLENGEKIDS

RED ALERT!

> The Passover is a celebration of remembering. It's a way of remembering how the Israelite people escaped from slavery in Egypt. Jesus was killed on the Passover. He too led us out of slavery—a slavery to sin.

#FORGIVINGCHALLENGEKIDS

DAY 35
THE STEP-UP: SANCTIFICATION
FORGIVENESS MOVES AT DIFFERENT SPEEDS

KEEP MOVING FORWARD

Climbing a mountain is not the same every day. There are three different ways that mountain climbers get to the top: hiking, belaying, and ice climbing.

- **HIKING**: In the beginning, a lot of time is spent hiking slowly but steadily uphill to high ground for hours upon hours. You must have lots of patience to get through this.

- **BELAYING**: To get over rock walls, mountain climbers use ropes, bolts, and anchors to pull themselves up the mountainside in pairs. This is called "belaying." You must be skilled and knowledgeable to get up the mountain rocks this way.

- **ICE CLIMBING**: A final way that climbers get up the mountain is ice climbing. This is the most dangerous of all. In the early days of ice climbing, people would have to use special tools that cut deep into the ice to make footholds, all while pressing up against its side with nothing but a long drop below.

You must be very brave to climb up ice. But little by little, you make your way up until you get to the beautiful view at the top! Climbers go through hours and days of struggle for the view. Sometimes it's boring and you just plod along steadily.

Other times, it's tricky and you move skillfully. And other times it's very dangerous and you must move very lightly and slowly.

GETTING TO THE TOP

A wonderful thing about forgiveness is that it can give us a brand-new outlook. It's like reaching the top of a mountain in that way. When we forgive, we have a fresh chance to see things in a different way.

It may be difficult to 'fess up, clean up, rise up, and step up, but God knows that all of the hard work is worth it. Without forgiveness, we are going to miss some beautiful views in life. Forgiveness keeps us moving forward.

Like hiking, belaying, and ice climbing, forgiveness is hard work. Jesus doesn't just encourage us to forgive—He demands it—even if we feel the hurt multiple times a day. After someone apologizes and you forgive them, it might take a while for the sting or deep cut to heal.

Also, forgiving others isn't a one-time thing. As it says in Luke 17:3-4, **"If your brother or sister sins against you, rebuke them; and if they repent, forgive them. Even if they sin against you seven times in a day and seven times come back to you saying 'I repent,' you must forgive them."**

God forgives us in the same way. Even if we come to Him seven times in a day to confess our sins, He will forgive us seven times. His love and patience and forgiveness are endless. So do the same with others—with Jesus's help.*

Jesus helps us to not give up when forgiveness seems to take too long or get too hard. So keep climbing, keep moving one small step at a time, and you will reach the top. There, you can plant the flag of forgiveness.

CHALLENGE

When does forgiveness feel like **hiking**: slow, steady work for hours and hours?

___

When does forgiveness feel like **belaying**; it's tricky and you need skill and knowledge to accomplish it?

___

When does forgiveness feel like **ice climbing**: extremely hard work for very tiny progress? (It can even seem dangerous and scary.)

___

God uses all things, including the hard times, to work for your good. The going may be tough, slow, or even tricky, but when you step up there is something beautiful at the end.

What beautiful view do you think God has for you at the end of each step?

FORGIVENESS: HIKING	FORGIVENESS: BELAYING	FORGIVENESS: ICE CLIMBING

*NOTE: Despite the call to forgiveness, remember that abuse is a terrible thing that needs to be stopped and should not be tolerated. Please talk to a trusted adult if you feel that someone is hurting you over and over. (For more information on this, please refer to the Letter to Facilitators on page 270.)

#FORGIVINGCHALLENGEKIDS

RED ALERT!

Noah's ark came to rest on "the mountains of Ararat," says Genesis 8:4. Today, Mount Ararat is found in modern-day Turkey. It has two volcanic cones—Greater Ararat and Little Ararat.

#FORGIVINGCHALLENGEKIDS

DAY 36
THE STEP-UP: SANCTIFICATION
FORGIVENESS MAKES US DIFFERENT

STRANGER IN A STRANGE LAND

If you have ever traveled to a different country, you know what it feels like to be a foreigner.

- You most likely won't speak the language. You won't be able to read posted signs and understand directions.

- You will not know what types of food to order on the menu.

- You may stand out if your clothing is different.

- A foreigner is not able to vote, not able to participate in all local activities, and is usually only allowed to stay for a limited period of time.

In the Bible, Christians are called foreigners. As it says in 1 Peter 2:11-12:

> "Dear friends, I urge you, as foreigners and exiles, to abstain from sinful desires, which wage war against your soul. Live such good lives among the pagans that, though they accuse you of doing wrong, they may see your good deeds and glorify God on the day he visits us."

God loves to use people who are different to carry out His plans. He used lowly and meek Mary and Joseph to be the mother and father for baby Jesus. He invited simple fishermen from Galilee to be His disciples. (Galileans were often viewed as "backward" country folk.) Jesus even told a parable called the Good Samaritan, which showed that outsiders can do heroic things. (Samaritans were hated "foreigners" to the Jewish people.)

When Jesus calls us foreigners, He is saying that our true kingdom, our true home, is in Heaven. If Earth is all there is, forgiveness doesn't make a whole lot of sense. Why spend time loving someone who is your enemy?

But as Christians, we understand that God created all people and wants to redeem all people—even our enemies. We also know that we are all sinful. Because we have all messed up, Jesus came and died for every single one of us.

Forgiveness makes us different because:

- We don't have to try to fit in with everyone.

- We can see ourselves as God sees us—as people who mess up and need to be rescued. When we forgive our enemy, it's a gift from one messed-up person to another.

- We don't have to get mad about every little problem because we know we have a heavenly home.

DON'T GET TOO COZY

When you visit a new land, it can be exciting—but most likely you will not feel completely at home. That's because it isn't your home. And when you return from a long trip, you appreciate the familiar feeling of home when you step through the door.

It's like that in this world. If Heaven is our home, we won't ever get too cozy here. As forgiven people, we won't always fit in with the crowd. But being a "foreigner" in this world helps us learn to forgive. When someone hurts us, we don't have to hold grudges because we're just passing through on our journey home. And when we finally arrive in Heaven and step through that door, we'll feel as if we are truly home.

CHALLENGE

Fill out the Mad Lib below with a friend or family member. Without reading the story to your friend, first ask him or her to provide a word that fits each of the things in parentheses—a mode of transportation, a foreign country, a famous tourist attraction, etc. Then plug those words into the story and read it aloud. It's fun to imagine what we might do if we went to a foreign country. But take time to thank God that we have a home in Heaven waiting for us.

MY DAY AS A FOREIGNER

Last summer, I took a _____ and arrived in the country of
(mode of transportation)

_____. As the conductor took my ticket, he told me to watch out
(name of a foreign country)

for _____ _____.
   (adjective)   (plural noun)

The first thing I wanted to see was _____ so I _____
                                    (a famous tourist attraction)   (verb)

onto the _____. But I forgot to exchange my dollars for
         (mode of transportation)

_____ so I didn't have any way to pay. I decided to _____
  (plural noun)   (verb)

the _____ miles instead.
      (number)

#FORGIVINGCHALLENGEKIDS

On the way I stopped at a _____ cafe to grab a _____
                            (adjective)   (noun)
to eat. But I couldn't read the menu and ended up ordering a _____.
                                                                      (noun)
When I finally arrived, I didn't know how to ask someone to take my picture, so

I decided to act it out. Instead of taking my picture, they thought I needed to

_____ the police. It took me a lot of _____ to get out
   (verb)   (-ing verb)
of that mess. When I finally _____ at the hotel, the manager informed
                                 (verb)
me that the only room left was the _____ room.
                                      (adjective)
I was so _____ that I wanted to _____.
            (an emotion)   (verb)
My day as a foreigner was certainly a _____ one!
                                         (adjective)

RED ALERT!

Mount Zion has many different meanings in the Bible. In 2 Samuel 5:7, Zion is the city of David. Sometimes, Zion is used to describe the City of our God on a high mountain. (Psalm 48:1-3). Mount Zion is also used to speak of the Temple...or the entire land of Israel... or a hill in west Jerusalem.

DAY 37
THE STEP-UP: SANCTIFICATION
FORGIVENESS IS NOT A SOLO CLIMB

WE ARE NOT ALONE

Edmund Hillary and Tenzing Norgay get all the credit for being the first men to climb the summit of Mount Everest. But if you asked them, they would say it took a whole team.

The expedition was set up by a British man named John Hunt long before Edmund and Tenzing were ever part of the group. Hunt, a military man, had been planning the expedition for years and years. To make it to the top, three tons of equipment had to be carried up the side of the mountain in small stages. Three tons is about as much as an African elephant! So think of it as carrying an elephant up the side of the mountain. In all, 350 porters, 20 Sherpas (local people in the Himalayan mountains), and 10 climbers were part of the expedition. That's quite a crew!

Each member of the team was carefully picked for their talent and knowledge. In addition to being climbers, many team members had other jobs like doctor, mechanic, and scientist. While up on Everest, they tested equipment, made important records of the land and weather, and even researched how the human body changes while climbing. Their discoveries would help future climbers.

As you travel on this journey of life, you may sometimes feel like a foreigner—you may feel different—but you are not alone. You have fellow travelers to give you support and encouragement. God made us to be in relationships with others. So we must stay attached to other believers as we follow Jesus. Working together, we can help each other keep from falling.

ROPE TEAMS

Alpine mountaineers rarely climb "solo," which means they rarely climb alone. A group of mountaineers is called a "rope team" because each person is connected to the others with ropes to keep the whole team safe.

This is also how Christians see themselves. Just like the first Everest team, everyone on Jesus's team plays a different role. We all have different challenges and tasks, but we have to stick together.

In the Book of Romans, Paul uses the idea of body parts working together to capture this idea.

> **"The body we're talking about is Christ's body of chosen people. Each of us finds our meaning and function as a part of his body. But as a chopped-off finger or cut-off toe we wouldn't amount to much, would we? So since we find ourselves fashioned into all these excellently formed and marvelously functioning parts in Christ's body, let's just go ahead and be what we were made to be, without enviously or pridefully comparing ourselves with each other, or trying to be something we aren't."**
> **Romans 12:4b-6 (The Message)**

When we start comparing ourselves to others or taking all of the credit instead of working together, it slows down our journey. Working together as a group will help you keep moving when little bumps, stings, and even deep cuts occur.

Forgiveness keeps the body of Christ together and working as one. It keeps us committed to one another.

COMMITMENTS AND COVENANTS

In *Being Challenge Kids*, we learned how forming friendships is so important in our journey. When Jesus picked His disciples, He was committed to them, no matter what happened. He does the same for you and me. He makes a covenant to stick with us through thick and thin.

Because Jesus is committed to us and loves us, we now are able to love others. This is made clear in 1 Peter 4:8-11 in The Message.

> **"Most of all, love each other as if your life depended on it. Love makes up for practically anything. Be quick to give a meal to the hungry, a bed to the homeless—cheerfully. Be generous with the different things that God gave you, passing them around so all get in on it: if words, let it be God's words; if help, let it be God's hearty help. That way, God's bright presence will be evident in everything through Jesus, and he'll get all the credit as the One mighty in everything—encores to the end of time."**

Without everyone doing their job, Edmund Hillary and Tenzing Norgay would never have reached the top. When we work together as Christians, we can love and serve the world together. God promises us that His presence will be with us, so you never go alone in this journey of following Jesus. We've got each other's backs, knowing that God is the leader of our "rope team." He's the one who keeps us from falling.

#FORGIVINGCHALLENGEKIDS

CHALLENGE

You are connected to all Christians around the world, but you also have a smaller "rope team" in your life. Your rope team is made up of the people whom you are around every day. This may be your family, church, small group, or class.

1 Think about who is on your rope team. Write those people or the name of your church in the spaces below.

2 How can you lend a hand to your rope team this week? Write your ideas beside the rope.

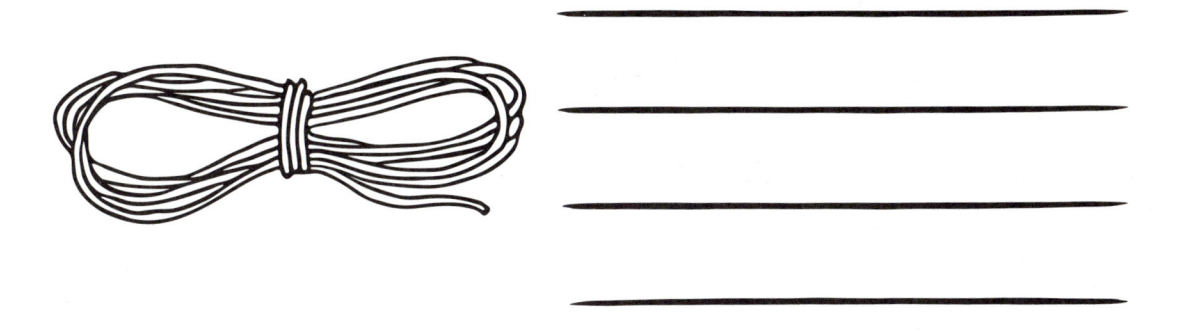

THE STEP-UP • 237

DAY 38
THE STEP-UP: SANCTIFICATION
LOVE YOUR ENEMIES

SIGNPOSTS

On the signpost below, fill in the distance that these famous mountains are from where you live. (Use a GPS app on a phone or tablet to calculate the distances.) On the blank sign, fill in your own favorite mountain.

- MOUNT EVEREST
- MOUNT FUJI
- MONT BLANC
- EL CAPITAN
- MOUNT OLYMPUS

Most mountains have mileage markers, signposts, or signals to let you know where to start. Some are carved in stone, while others are made of wood or metal. There are also signs to let you know when you have reached the peak or certain places on the mountain.

When you are on the path to forgiveness, you receive signs as well. For instance, if you feel anger at something that someone has done to you, that is a sign that you're facing a choice between two paths. You can choose to respond with vengeance or you can choose to respond with forgiveness.

Which way you go can make all the difference in your life—and other people's lives.

THE FORGIVING BISHOP

Les Miserables, by Victor Hugo, is one of the greatest novels ever written about forgiveness. In this classic story, Jean Valjean serves nineteen years in prison for stealing a loaf of bread. When he's finally released, no one will give him shelter because he was once a criminal.

However, a kindly bishop welcomes Jean Valjean into his house, feeds him, and gives him a place to stay. How does Jean Valjean respond to this kindness? He steals the bishop's precious silverware and slips away in the night. When Jean is arrested and hauled back to the bishop, the bishop faced a fork in the road. He could respond to Jean Valjean with bitterness, or he could respond with love. He was at a crossroads. Which sign would he follow?

The bishop told the policeman that Jean Valjean could keep the silver, and he asked that the man be released. What's more, he told Jean Valjean that he forgot to take the candlesticks, which were very valuable.

When he was given the candlesticks, Jean Valjean nearly fainted. Then the kindly bishop said in a low voice, "Do not forget, ever, that you promised me to use this silver to become an honest man."

And so it happened. Because of the love shown by the bishop, Jean Valjean became an honest man. He still faced many troubles, but the bishop's forgiveness and God's forgiveness transformed him forever.

This story sounds a lot like the words of Jesus in Matthew 5, when He said that if someone steals your shirt, give him your coat as well. Then Jesus goes on to say, **"You have heard that it was said, 'Love your neighbor and hate your enemy.' But I tell you, love your enemies and pray for those who persecute you, that you may be children of your Father in heaven."**

It probably wasn't easy for the bishop to forgive the man who stole from him. When he learned that the man whom he fed and sheltered had stolen his silver, the bishop felt pain and sorrow. But that's a normal part of the forgiving process. You have to feel pain to forgive. After all, if you haven't been hurt by someone, you wouldn't have anything to forgive. The moment the pain begins, you are already on the journey of forgiveness.

PAUSE FOR PRAYER

Some people say, "Good people won't have enemies. They are friends with everyone." But the Bible says there will be times when you'll have enemies, no matter how good you may be. After all, even Jesus had enemies.

One of the most important tools in learning to forgive is prayer. In the *Being Challenge Kids* book, we learned how Pausing for Prayer can help us connect with God. It can also help us reconnect with others. The wonderful thing is that when you pray for someone, your feelings about that person will begin to change.

Jesus says we become who God created us to be when we pray for our enemies.

If you're working on forgiveness and not sure if you're making any progress, Ephesians 4:32 is a great Bible verse to use.

> **"Be kind to one another, tenderhearted, forgiving one another, as God in Christ forgave you." Ephesians 4:32**

This is groundbreaking! It's the total opposite of getting even. Prayer helps us reach this guidepost. With prayer, you can begin to put into practice what Paul talked about in Ephesians.

CHALLENGE

Write the verse Ephesians 4:32 on the sign at the summit of the mountain. If you have someone who feels like an enemy in your life, try praying for them for a whole week. See what God can do with a simple prayer request.

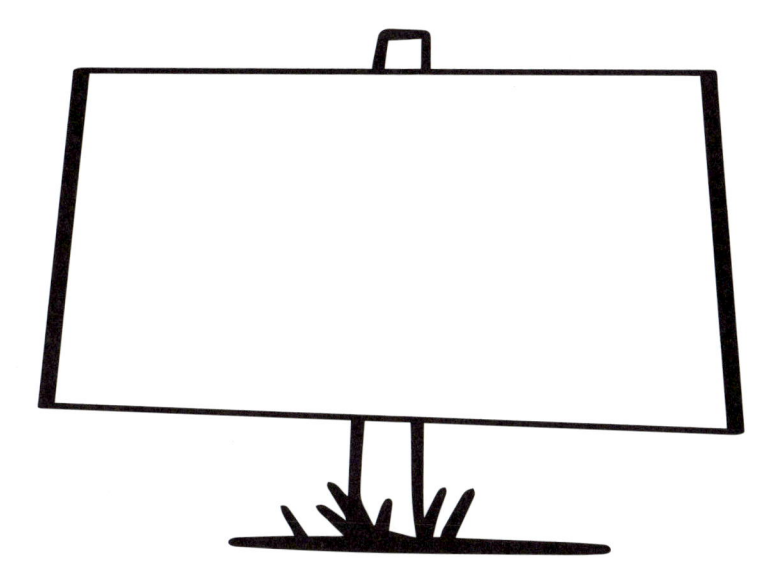

DAY 39

THE STEP-UP SANCTIFICATION

FORGIVENESS FREES YOU TO HELP OTHERS

WHAT IS THE 'EVEREST' IN YOUR LIFE?

As Edmund Hillary was climbing Mount Everest, he would pass villages of the Sherpa people of Nepal and notice children with no shoes and sick people with no one to care for them. He saw kids without schools and little food to eat. When he asked one man what he could do to help, the man said he could build a school in one of the villages.

So Edmund decided he wanted to spend his life helping the Sherpa people. He started the Himalayan Trust and built many schools and hospitals in Nepal. Climbing Everest made Edmund famous, but he accomplished so much more than simply climbing a mountain. He started a program that helped entire villages and hundreds of lives.

Like Edmund Hillary, we all have our own "Everests" or challenges to climb. God promises He will never leave us and that He will use us to help others.

> "He comes alongside us when we go through hard times, and before you know it, he brings us alongside someone else who is going through hard times so that we can be there for that person just as God was there for us. We have plenty of hard times that come from following the Messiah,

but no more so than the good times of his healing comfort—we get a full measure of that, too." 2 Corinthians 1:4-5 (The Message)

In addition to forgiving us, Jesus invites us to help others discover that they too can be forgiven. Our hard times can be used by God to help others just like Edmund's climb helped the Sherpa people. <u>Forgiveness offers you an opportunity to step up and help others along the way.</u>

Without forgiveness in your life, your heart would be weighed down by so much baggage that it would be difficult to help anyone else. Forgiveness doesn't just give you eyes to see the hurts in others. It frees your hands to lift others up.

FROM BLUNDER TO BOULDER

Many people remember Peter for his biggest blunder. He was the disciple who denied Jesus three times just before the crucifixion. Peter was afraid the Romans might arrest him and crucify him alongside Jesus, so he was terrified.

Peter was crushed with grief at what he had done—denying his Lord when Jesus needed His friends most.

Fortunately, Peter's story didn't end there. In the last chapter of the Book of John—chapter 21—we read how Peter and other disciples went back to fishing on the Sea of Galilee. All night, they caught no fish. But in the morning, a man on the shore told them to throw their net on the right side of the boat. When they did, their nets overflowed with fish! That's when the disciple John noticed who the man on the shore was—Jesus!

Immediately, Peter threw on his coat, hurled himself into the water, and swam for shore. There, Jesus was waiting for him, cooking fish over a charcoal fire.

On that beach, Jesus turned Peter's life completely around.

Three times, Jesus asked Peter if he loved Him. Three times, Peter said yes. Peter had denied Jesus three times at the crucifixion. But now, as if to erase each of those denials, Peter says, "I love you" three times to Jesus.

The forgiveness that Peter received on the beach that day made him a new man. He went on to live up to his nickname, the "rock" or "big boulder." He preached the message of Jesus, helping others find freedom and forgiveness in the Lord. The church, in the early days, grew quickly from 120 to 3,120! (Acts 2:41)

As Peter's story shows, being forgiven gives us opportunities to show forgiveness to others, and to receive it. This is the beautiful view you have been climbing for, when those hateful or sad feelings are gone. We are set up to STEP UP.

CHALLENGE

Look for an opportunity to help someone else outside the rope team that you identified on Day 37. You may even want to invite members of your rope team to serve with you. Notice those around you, like Edmund Hillary did with the people of Nepal.

What do they need? _____

How can you help them? _____

How does forgiveness help you see others in need? _____

#FORGIVINGCHALLENGEKIDS

RED ALERT!

When Peter denied Jesus three times, he did it beside a charcoal fire (John 18). When Jesus forgave Peter on the beach, he did it beside another charcoal fire (John 21). Jesus recreated Peter's worst moment and turned it into his best moment—his moment of forgiveness and freedom.

#FORGIVINGCHALLENGEKIDS

DAY 40
THE STEP-UP: SANCTIFICATION
FORGIVENESS: THE BEST PRIZE OF ALL

THE CLAW GAME
Match each claw with the correctly shaped item that it can pick up.

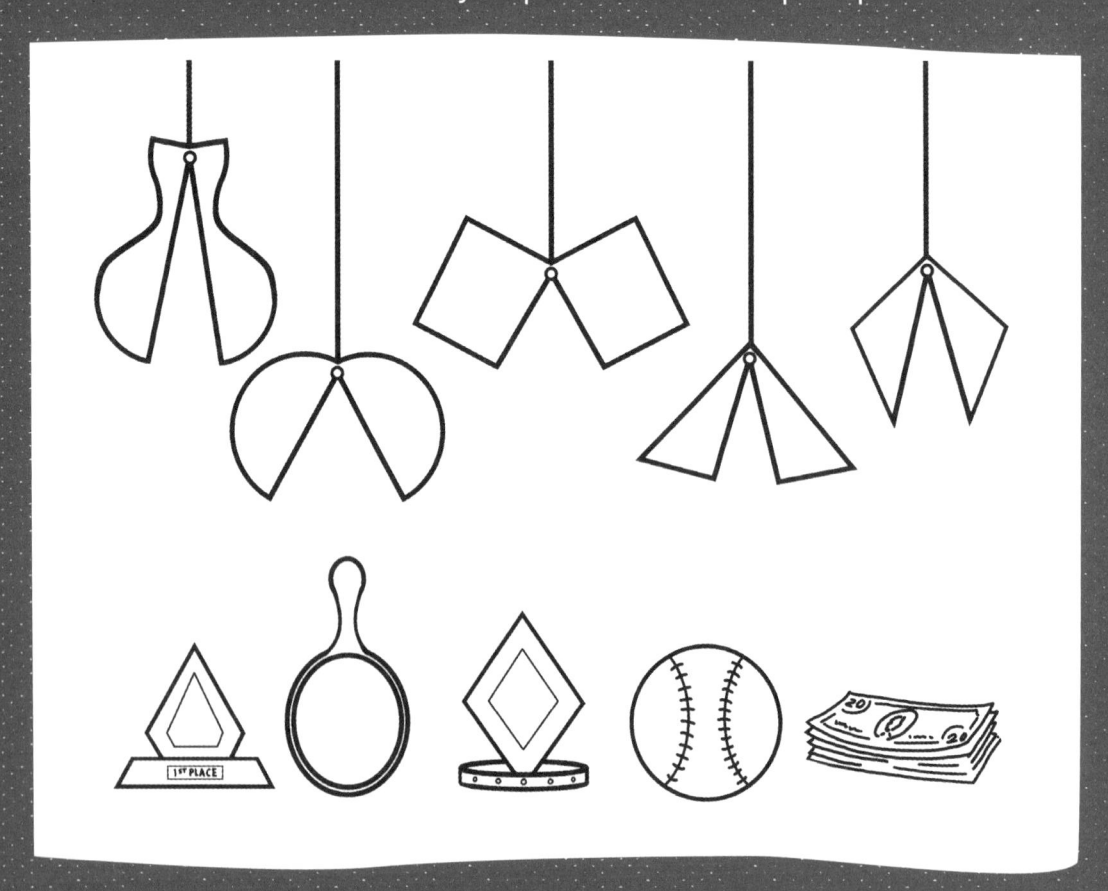

LIAM AND THE CLAW

Liam pressed his face against the cold glass of the claw machine, his final ticket held tightly in his hand. The fluorescent lights and peppy music from the arcade were so vibrant at first, but now it seemed loud and blaring, making him feel nauseous. This was his last chance.

The pit in Liam's stomach grew bigger as he thought of the money he owed his friends. He borrowed money to play the claw game, and he was so sure he would win that he didn't worry about the money he was spending. What's a couple bucks here or there?

But the little amounts added up to one big debt, and now he was in over his head. He owed $50 to his friends.

Liam could sense his little brother, Noah, hovering behind him.

"Liam, let me do this." Noah said. "I can get a prize. Besides, I'm better at the claw machine than you are."

Liam's pride was stung by this comment. No one likes to be beat by his little brother, but his anxiety was greater than his pride. In desperation, he handed over his final ticket.

"I'm going to the bathroom," Liam mumbled as he heard the machine greedily suck in his last chance. He couldn't stand by and watch.

When Liam returned from the bathroom, he expected the worst. But he found Noah beaming at him with a huge smile.

"We won, Liam! We won!" Noah yelled.

Liam froze in his tracks. He refused to believe it. But what exactly had they won? Liam still owed his friends $50, and a stuffed animal or even the smaller prizes wouldn't cover that.

How would you respond if you were Liam and were told you're a winner? To answer that question, you would first need to know what it is that you won. We'll get to that part of the story later. But first…

CANCELED DEBTS

Jesus uses debt to explain forgiveness and how it helps us understand God's love. The story goes like this:

> "**Jesus said to him,** 'Simon, I have something to tell you.'
> "'**Oh? Tell me.**'
> "'Two men were in debt to a banker. One owed five hundred silver pieces, the other fifty. Neither of them could pay up, and so the banker canceled both debts. Which of the two would be more grateful?'
> "**Simon answered, 'I suppose the one who was forgiven the most.'**
> "'That's right,' **said Jesus."** Luke 7:40-43a (The Message)

The man in Jesus's story was forgiven five hundred pieces of silver, which is about $50,000 in today's money. Can you imagine winning that much money? But in Jesus, you've won even more: You have hit the ultimate jackpot!

When Jesus forgave you, He washed you clean from all your sin and debt. That's far more than $50,000. That's priceless. Now, back to our story…

#FORGIVINGCHALLENGEKIDS

THE JACKPOT

With his eyes shining, Noah showed Liam the prize. He held up a stack of twenty dollar bills, wrapped in brightly colored paper. "Five hundred dollars, Liam! Five hundred! We got the jackpot!"

Liam rushed over to hug his brother and hold the prize in his hand. He couldn't believe it was real.

Liam was able to pay back what he owed, and he still had $450 left over. He decided he no longer wanted to spend money at the arcade, and the first $50 went into the offering at church. Liam used $200 to buy a lawnmower and started a lawn-mowing business. He also gave his little brother $100 of the prize money for a new video game console he was saving up for. Finally Liam put the last $50 in savings.

MY CUP OVERFLOWS

God has paid in full for you. But He didn't just cancel your debt. He gave you above and beyond what you need. The Bible says that God fills us so much that extra spills out all over.

> **"My cup overflows. Surely your goodness and love will follow me all the days of my life, and I will dwell in the house of the Lord forever."
> Psalm 23:5b-6**

Here is what STEPPING UP looks like after forgiveness:

- We can look back and see the good God has done, even in the bad times.
- We don't have to give up when the going gets tough.
- We will be okay, even if we don't fit in with everyone else.

- We won't ever go alone on our journey because we have our church and other believers alongside us.

- We can extend a helping hand to others in need, even if they are our worst enemy.

- Because you won the jackpot, you are able to step up into the plans God has for you.

CHALLENGE

How can you step up into what God has for you? The first way is to make a plan.

GOAL: _____

I can accomplish this goal by following these steps:

STEP 3: _____

STEP 2: _____

STEP 1: _____

I need the following people to help me achieve my goal:

_____

_____

I hope to reach my goal by _____ (date).

Name _____ Date _____

#FORGIVINGCHALLENGEKIDS

RED ALERT!

The Mount of Olives is where Jesus wept in the Garden of Gethsemane. It's also a place of glory. Ezekiel had a vision of God's glory on the mountain east of Jerusalem—probably the Mount of Olives (Ezekiel 11:23). In Acts 1:6-12, the resurrected Jesus said goodbye to His disciples and ascended into Heaven at the Mount of Olives.

#FORGIVINGCHALLENGEKIDS

WHAT NOW?

Congratulations! You have arrived at the end of *Forgiving Challenge Kids*. You've come a long way over the past 40 days. You've gone through the Mess-up, the 'Fess-up, the Clean-up, the Rise-up, and the Step-up.

Each week, you dug deeper and went a little further in your exploration of forgiveness. But throughout the challenge there was one word that kept coming up over the entire 40 days. Did you see it? (Hint: "Come on, catch up!")

The word that was used over and over was UP.

The word "up" was first used in the English language before the 12th Century, and it meant "to move to a higher place." Throughout the entire Bible, God's plan has always been to take us up from where we are to a higher place.

UP IN THE OLD TESTAMENT

God told Noah He would save him UP out of the water with an ark.

God told Abraham to look UP at the stars because He promised him generations of children, as numerous as the stars. (One of those descendants would be Jesus.)

Isaac was brought UP on a mountain, where he was rescued from being the sacrifice.

Moses brought the people UP out of Egypt from slavery and into the Promised Land.

Moses went UP a mountain to get the Ten Commandments, the rules that would set apart the Israelites from everyone else.

In Psalms, King David wrote, **"I lift UP my eyes to the mountains— where does my help come from? My help comes from the Lord, the Maker of heaven and earth. Psalm 121:1-2**

Even after the Israelites disobeyed God and found themselves back in slavery, God sent prophets and kings to help them. From the beginning, God had promised to rescue them. As they waited, the prophet Isaiah wrote that a Savior would come. He said, **"A shoot will come UP from the stump of Jesse; from his roots a Branch will bear fruit." Isaiah 11:1**

As the Israelites waited for the Messiah, they looked for a mighty ruler to teach them. **"Many nations will come and say, 'Come, let us go UP to the mountain of the Lord, to the temple of the God of Jacob. He will teach us his ways, so that we may walk in his paths.'" Micah 4:2**

UP IN THE NEW TESTAMENT

In order for us to look UP to God, Jesus had to first come down to us. What a glorious moment it must have been as the shepherds saw angels singing UP in the heavens.

WHAT NOW? • 253

As Jesus grew UP and started His ministry, He announced that He was here to rescue all men. He said, **"No one can come to me unless the Father who sent me draws them, and I will raise them UP at the last day. John 6:44**

Jesus the Messiah went UP to the city of Jerusalem on a lowly donkey. Jesus was taken UP on the hill of Golgotha and hung UP on a cross to die. This was not the high place that the people expected. They were picturing Jesus UP on a throne, or UP on a white horse going into battle.

Three days later, Jesus rose UP out of His tomb. He had defeated death!

After spending a few weeks with His disciples, Jesus's time on earth came to an end. **"When he had led them out to the vicinity of Bethany, he lifted UP his hands and blessed them. While he was blessing them, he left them and was taken UP into heaven." Luke 24:50-51**

The disciples were frozen, looking UP into the sky. What now?

An angel came and told the disciples they didn't have to keep staring UP at the sky. They had been raised UP and will have the Holy Spirit to go with them into all the world, making disciples of all nations.

Know this. When Jesus comes into your life, He always takes you UP from where you were to a higher place.

#FORGIVINGCHALLENGEKIDS

ONLY THE BEGINNING
Your forgiveness is the beginning of an invitation to follow Jesus.

When you have been forgiven by Jesus, you shouldn't be shocked when others MESS UP, because you have done the same. You will allow them to 'FESS UP, and you will help them CLEAN UP their messes. You also won't be afraid to ask others what you can do to CLEAN UP the messes you've made. You will have the strength to RISE UP again, and you will celebrate when others rise.

So what are you waiting for? STEP UP and be a part of God's forgiveness in the world.

You're still welcomed when you mess up.

You'll find a safe place to 'fess up.

Jesus did the clean-up for you,

So be ready to rise up and start anew.

It's time to step up to God's call,

Forgiveness…given freely for all.

HAVE FUN COLORING THIS PAGE!
FIND MORE LIKE THIS AT FORGIVINGCHALLENGE.COM/KIDS

THE MOUNTAINS OF REDVALE

PART 7

This was the big one.

The earlier eruption was just a baby blast compared to this explosion. As Mount Goel blew its top, spewing a geyser of green goo into the air, Isabella and the others were thrown from their feet.

Fortunately, they had gotten partially down the side of the mountain when the volcano erupted. If they hadn't, they would have been covered in ten feet of goo in seconds. But an avalanche of slime was rolling down the mountain, coming toward them like a monstrous green wave.

"Hurry, hurry, hurry!" Bob the Cave Whale yelled. "You'll be safe if you climb into my mouth!"

Isabella tried to scramble back to her feet, but every time she stood up, the earth shook again, and she was slammed against the ground. After one of the biggest jolts yet, she lost her balance and tumbled down a very steep slope. She did a complete flip, over and over and over again, rolling down the mountain, wildly out of control. She bounced off of a rock, which sent her sprawling in a different direction.

Although she was rolling away from the slime, she was also moving farther away from Bob and the others. She tried to grab onto a rock as she continued to slide down the slope, but it was just out of reach. Finally, she smashed into a small tree, coming to a painful stop.

"Ouch." Her ribs hurt. Her right shoulder hurt. Her left ankle hurt. More parts of her body hurt than didn't.

Rising to her feet, she looked up the slope, hoping to see Bob the Cave Whale racing to her rescue. But all she saw was a quickly advancing blob of slime. She didn't think she was going to be able to outrun it, so she began to climb the tree that she had slammed into. It was her only hope.

TRAPPED BY A ROCK!

Meanwhile, Aiden and Emily were also hurled down a steep slope. They too tumbled and crashed and bounced and bashed into things, sliding and flipping down the side of the mountain. Even worse, they knocked loose some rocks, causing a small landslide—which became a big landslide.

"AHHHHHHH!"

It was like being caught in a stampede of rocks and dirt and dust. Aiden felt as if the entire side of the mountain was sliding downhill, carrying him and Emily along with it. When the slope finally leveled off, the two Perez kids found themselves partially buried in rocks of all sizes.

"My foot is stuck!" Aiden shouted. He tried to yank it free, but the bottom half of his right leg was wedged under a stone too heavy for him to move.

Emily's head was spinning like a top. She sat up and waited for the world to stop twirling around in her mind. Then she shook her head, dusted herself off, and leaped to her feet. A pain shot through her ankle, and she collapsed back to the ground.

"What's wrong?" Aiden asked. "Why aren't you pushing this rock off of me?"

"I think I sprained my ankle."

Emily looked up the mountain, where the slime was oozing its way down the slope. It would be upon them in no time. But she had to try to help Aiden, sprained ankle or not. So she got back up and hopped over to him. Then she put all of her weight behind the rock and pushed.

Nothing. Emily didn't have the strength to move the rock. But she tried again. And again. And again. The rock was immovable, but the slime wasn't. She looked up to see that the slime almost upon them. They were doomed.

#FORGIVINGCHALLENGEKIDS

TRAPPED IN A TREE!

Meanwhile, Red, Malachi, Frankie, and Chloe were riding inside Bob the Cave Whale's wide-open mouth. Even Balthazar the donkey had climbed inside. It was like being in a speedboat as the whale raced down the slope.

Off to their right, they could see Aiden trapped under a boulder, while Emily tried to push it off. To their left, Isabella was trapped in a tree. The slime had already reached her, and it was pushing against the tree, which looked like it was about to crack.

Who to rescue first?

"Let Chloe and me out, so we can help Aiden and Emily," Frankie said. "Then you guys go save Isabella while we rescue our friends."

"But you'll never be able to get that boulder off of him," Red said.

"My brother is stronger than he looks," said Chloe.

"Hey!" Frankie said, giving Chloe a playful push. "I look strong!"

"Frankie, I think your idea is the best one we got," Malachi said. "Bob! Drop them off!"

The Cave Whale skidded to a stop, giving Frankie and Chloe time to hop out and sprint to the aid of the two Perez kids. Then Bob wheeled around and jetted toward Isabella, who was perched on a branch that looked like it was about to break. Slime jammed into the tree, threatening to tear it out by its roots.

"Turn your ear to me, Lord, come quickly to our rescue!" Malachi shouted as they closed in on Isabella. "Be our rock of refuge, a strong fortress to save us. In your hands, we commit our spirit; deliver us, Lord, our faithful God!"

Bob the Cave Whale plowed directly through the slime, hurling waves of ooze to both sides. Then, with a loud SNAP, the branch that Isabella was sitting on broke in half. She fell with it.

"HEEEEEELP!"

THE WINDS OF CHANGE

Back on the other side of the slope, Frankie, Chloe, and Emily put their combined strength behind the rock on top of Aiden's leg. They felt like they were trying to move an entire mountain.

"YAHHHHHH!" Frankie gave out a battle cry as he threw his shoulder against the boulder. At last, it began to budge.

"Don't let up!" Aiden shouted. "It's working!"

Aiden felt the pinching pressure on his leg begin to let up. He could wiggle his leg, but could he pull it from underneath the rock?

"Is your foot loose?" Frankie called. "I don't know if I can hold this much longer!"

Aiden realized that if he untied his shoelaces and yanked his foot out of his shoe, he might just break free.

"Hurry!"

"That did it!" Aiden shouted.

His foot slid out of his shoe, and he tugged his leg free just as Frankie's strength gave out.

Aiden quickly scooted backward, free of the boulder. His right leg ached, but he thought he could hop to safety on one foot. Frankie threw an arm around his shoulder, giving him support. His ankle throbbed with every hop. Emily's ankle was also in pain, so Chloe put an arm around her shoulder as well, acting as a crutch.

Off in the distance, Aiden could see Bob the Cave Whale racing in their direction. But looking at the approaching wall of slime, Aiden realized that Bob wasn't going to reach them in time. The slime was almost on top of them. They were about to be completely buried in gunk.

"I don't think we're going to make it," Chloe said.

"Gotta keep trying," Frankie said, with Aiden leaning against him for support.

The slime was about five feet away when a mighty wind came out of nowhere. It reminded them of the wind that struck their city during the last hurricane

#FORGIVINGCHALLENGEKIDS

season. The wind not only knocked the kids off of their feet, but it appeared to be holding back the slime. The wall of goo came to a sudden and surprising stop, about three feet away from the kids.

That wasn't all.

The slime suddenly began to change color, from green to crystal clear. And as the wind continued to flow over the slime, the goo began to thin out. Large chunks of slime went flying away, shattering into a million drops of water.

The slime was being transformed into water—pure, living water. What's more, the side of the mountain was also transforming. It was changing from gray and brown to green. But this wasn't the green of slime. This was the green of grass. There were other colors as well—red, violet, orange, and yellow—as an army of flowers sprouted up and down the face of the mountain.

"What just happened?" Frankie said. One second, he was helping Aiden hobble to safety, while a mountain of slime threatened to cover them. The next second, they were standing in a field of flowers with streams of clear water running beside them, like silver threads.

"You guys just happened," said Malachi.

Hearing Malachi's voice, Emily spun around to see that Bob the Cave Whale had arrived. Malachi, Red, and Balthazar were all sitting inside his open mouth, while Isabella was perched on his back, safe and sound.

"I don't understand," Frankie said. "What do you mean WE just happened?"

"All of you STEPPED UP," Malachi said, as he climbed out of the whale's mouth. "You've been sanctified."

"Santa-fied?" said Chloe. "You mean we've been changed into Santas?"

"Sanctified, not Santa-fied," said Malachi. "Sanctified means you've been set apart. You're different because of the forgiveness you showed to one another. And when you are changed, the world of Redvale has a knack for changing too."

"Because of what you did for each other—risking your lives—the Winds of Redvale blew strong and clear," said Balthazar. "The slime was changed into rivers of living water. And the barren land became clothed in grass and flowers."

THE GOOD LAND

Isabella stared down from Bob's back, taking in the miracle of what had just happened. As she did, a Bible verse she once memorized popped into her head. She stood up on Bob's back and felt the urge to shout it out.

"For the Lord your God is bringing you into a good land—a land with brooks, streams, and deep springs gushing out into the valleys and hills; a land with wheat and barley, vines and fig trees, pomegranates, olive oil and honey; a land where bread will not be scarce and you will lack nothing; a land where the rocks are iron and you can dig copper out of the hills."

After Isabella finished speaking, Malachi completed the verse from the Book of Deuteronomy. "When you have eaten and are satisfied, praise the Lord your God for the good land he has given you. Be careful that you do not forget the Lord your God…He led you through the vast and dreadful wilderness."

Rejoicing, they all climbed back into Bob's wide-open mouth—including Isabella, who slid down from his back. Then the Cave Whale took off, racing down the side of Mount Goel, leaping into the air and skimming across the surface of the streams. It was the best ride Isabella had ever experienced.

When they reached the bottom of the mountain, they came to a wide, open field of flowers, where a large red tent had been raised. Isabella's heart began to race.

"Has the King come?" she asked.

"The King sent the wind," Malachi said. "So yes, he is here. He would like to meet the two newcomers."

All eyes turned to Frankie and Chloe. The two kids blushed and bowed their heads.

As they entered the tent, trumpeters on both sides began to play a fanfare. Isabella looked up to the roof of the tent where five banners were hung. On the banners were their names: Isabella, Aiden, Emily, Frankie, and Chloe. They had seen their names on banners before, but it seemed strange to see the names of their former enemies right next to theirs.

#FORGIVINGCHALLENGEKIDS

The King rose from his throne and approached. Isabella sensed a great and lasting comfort in his smile. His smile was like a cool breeze on a hot day.

"Look inside, and what we see is that anyone united with Jesus the Messiah gets a fresh start, is created new," the King declared. "The old life is gone; a new life emerges! Look at it! All this comes from the God who settled the relationship between us and him, and then called us to settle our relationships with each other."

"What's he talking about?" Frankie whispered to his sister.

"I'm talking about change," the King said. "All of you have been changed in ways you do not fully understand."

Then the King looked at Frankie and Chloe.

"Frankie and Chloe, you risked your lives for two people you once bullied. Frankie, you learned that you really like Aiden, even though you oppose each other in sports. You realized that you don't always have to be the best in soccer when you're the best of friends. And Chloe, you learned that people do like you once they get to know you. You don't have to hide behind the mask of a bully."

Then the King turned to Aiden and Emily.

"Aiden and Emily, you began this adventure seeking vengeance. But you learned that with vengeance, you do nothing but put yourself in an even deeper pit. You learned to be peacemakers."

The King looked out on the entire crowd.

"The peace between Frankie and Chloe and Emily and Aiden has also brought peace to Redvale. The land has been transformed!"

Finally, the king turned toward Isabella, who lowered her eyes.

"And Isabella, you have taken the first big step toward repairing your broken friendship with Nova. You realized your sin, and you have decided to mend the break. You still have a long, difficult climb ahead of you. But if you've shown anything on this adventure, it's that you're good at climbing mountains."

The King motioned toward the back of the tent, where several women approached, carrying royal robes and several wrapped gifts.

"You're done with your old life," the King declared, turning back to the five kids. "It's like a filthy set of ill-fitting clothes you've removed and put in the fire. Now you're dressed in a new wardrobe. Every item of your new way of life is custom-made by the Creator, with his label on it."

With these words, the five heroes were fitted with royal robes.

"Cool," said Frankie, examining his sleeves. "This beats a new baseball uniform."

"Don't open your gifts until you return home," the King said, handing them each a wrapped package.

The rest of the day was spent sharing music, stories, and lots and lots of incredible food. Isabella loved it all, but there still seemed to be a sadness hanging over her. Balthazar must have sensed this because the donkey came up to her and nuzzled against her.

"Donkeys are not fast and flashy like horses," Balthazar said. "But we are good at carrying heavy loads. I wish I could carry your heavy burden, my daughter."

Isabella wiped a tear from her eye. "But what if Nova doesn't want to be my friend again?"

"That is difficult, I know. God in Heaven is saddened when His sons and daughters do not want to be His friends, so He knows what you're feeling. Go to Him with your worries. He'll listen."

Balthazar looked her straight in the eyes and added: "A donkey once had the honor of carrying a King on his back as he entered the city of Jerusalem. One week later, that King was killed. Then three days after that, the King rose from the dead. Life is all about the ups and downs—the valleys and mountains. You're in a valley now, but God can carry you back to the mountain."

Isabella smiled through the tears and recited a verse she knew by heart: "I look up to the mountains; does my strength come from mountains? No, my strength comes from God, who made heaven, and earth, and mountains."

#FORGIVINGCHALLENGEKIDS

A FRESH START

When night had fallen, Emily felt a cozy kind of happiness. With torches lighting up the darkness, everyone said their farewells. Malachi, Red, Bob the Cave Whale, Rockette, and even Doc Rock were all there to say goodbye to the five kids.

Then the kids entered a dark cave, one at a time…

…and suddenly found themselves back where they began. They were in Verne Park standing at the edge of a pit and wearing ordinary clothes once again. Time was still frozen as several kids stood like statues; they were in the middle of hurling buckets of slime on top of Frankie and Chloe, who were back at the bottom of the pit.

"Time is about to start back up," Emily said to Aiden. "You know what to do, don't you?"

As Aiden nodded, time unfroze. Emily and Aiden leaped into the pit, directly into the path of the slime that was being tossed on the heads of Frankie and Chloe. Emily felt the sticky goo slap her in the face, and it smelled horrific! Even Isabella leaped into the pit to keep the goo from hitting Frankie and Chloe.

The other kids stared down into the pit in complete confusion.

Emily, Aiden, and Isabella looked at all of the slime dripping from their faces, and they couldn't help but laugh out of pure joy.

The other kids, standing around the pit, stood there with mouths hanging open, as Frankie and Chloe gave fist bumps to the three Perez kids. Then the five new friends climbed out of the pit, and Chloe slapped an arm around Emily.

"Don't you think we should open our gifts?" Frankie asked, staring at the presents that were piled up on the ground.

"Yes, yes, let's open them!" Emily shouted, handing them out to Chloe, Frankie, Aiden, and Isabella.

They ripped off the wrapping like it was Christmas day, uncovering long, narrow boxes. Popping off the lids, a golden glow rose from each box like the rising sun. Inside the boxes were golden shovels—like the ones that Emily and Aiden had used to rescue Frankie and Chloe.

Emily held her shovel high, like a sword. "I think we know what these are for!"

The new friends shared a smile. And then, with renewed energy, they used their shovels to fill in the pit. As they did, several monarch butterflies came fluttering by, landing on their heads like crowns.

— THE END —

#FORGIVINGCHALLENGEKIDS

"I look up to the mountains; does my strength come from mountains? No, my strength comes from God, who made heaven, and earth, and mountains."

#FORGIVINGCHALLENGEKIDS

ABOUT THE AUTHORS

Zach Zehnder is a husband, father, speaker, author, and pastor. His life mission is to challenge people of all ages to become greater followers of Jesus. Zach continues to seek new and innovative ways to share the Gospel with the world, from raising money to buy a recovery house by breaking a Guinness World Record for the Longest Speech Marathon to paying for the church logo to be tattooed on church members. In 2017, Zach wrote the bestselling books *Red Letter Challenge* and *Being Challenge* and together with his wife Allison, co-wrote *Red Letter Challenge Kids* and *Forgiving Challenge Kids*. They co-founded a ministry under the name Red Letter Living and continue to write books and speak about the importance of following Jesus.

Allison Zehnder was raised in West Togo, Africa, as a missionary kid. Moving back to the United States, she graduated from Concordia University Wisconsin with a degree in Theology and minor in Missions and Youth Ministry. Along with Zach, she moved to Mount Dora, Florida, and served as Children's Director for 5 years at theCross. She is co-author of *Red Letter Challenge Kids* and *Being Challenge Kids* and currently assists in other writing projects for Red Letter Living. After 11 years in Florida, Zach and Allison moved back to Zach's childhood home in Omaha, NE, with their two sons, Nathan and Brady.

Doug Peterson is the Gold-Medallion-winning author of 72 books, including 42 for the popular VeggieTales series and five historical novels. He is the co-storywriter for the best-selling VeggieTales video, *Larry-Boy and the Rumor Weed*, and recently worked as head writer on six comic books in *The Legends of Lightfall* series. Doug has also been a writer for the University of Illinois since 1979, and he lives in Champaign, Illinois, with his wife, Nancy. They have two grown sons. You can find Doug online at bydougpeterson.com, or on Facebook under "Doug Peterson Author."

DEAR FACILITATOR,

In our introduction, we compared learning to forgive to climbing a big mountain. Traveling through this study, you will get the unique opportunity to hear about the different mountains that children will climb over. Some of them may be similar to what you have experienced in your past; others will be completely unique to them.

Some children are facing mountains that are bigger than anything any human should ever have to climb and are not equipped to scale these challenges alone. You cannot climb these mountains for them, but you do have a responsibility to be aware of when intervention is necessary. Abuse should never be tolerated.

If you believe that a child has disclosed abuse, please visit the website **ChildHelp.org** for the next steps. You are not responsible for follow-up care. Your job is to take that information to authorities. Please don't get personally involved in mediating the situation.

One of the best ways that you can create an environment where alleged abuse can be acknowledged and stopped is to be a **L.E.A.D.E.R.**, as described by Josh McDowell and Bob Hostetler in the *Handbook on Counseling Youth*.

1. LISTEN. Be slow to speak and quick to listen and believe.

2. EMPATHIZE. Don't lecture, but rather be someone the child can hurt with. Offer love and support.

3. AFFIRM. Tell them they did the right thing to talk about it. It's okay to say, "No."

4. DIRECT. Point the child to God as the source of healing and wholeness. Help the child turn the responsibility of the abuse from him- or herself onto the perpetrator and to realize that this process of healing and recovery will take time.

#FORGIVINGCHALLENGEKIDS

5. ENLIST. Allow the child to choose caring people who can encourage and offer a fuller support system. In most states, you must also enlist the involvement of law enforcement and social services. Rather than fearing these people's involvement, understand that they're trained professionals who, for the most part, care deeply about children.

6. REFER. Bring a professional Christian counselor into the situation. It's imperative to invite professionals into this very sensitive situation.

No matter if you are a parent, Sunday School leader, teacher, or another adult in this child's life, you have an important role. Thank you for your willingness to serve and help them along in their journey. Your position is so precious and needed.

Forgiveness is an ongoing process of learning, but thankfully we never go alone.

> **"And my God will supply every need of yours according to his riches in glory in Christ Jesus. To our God and Father be glory forever and ever. Amen."**
> **Philippians 4:19-20 (ESV)**

Allison Zehnder

Cynthia B. Wanberg, M.Ed, LMHC, NCC, RPT-S

DISCLAIMER

The contents of this book are for informational and educational purposes only. Nothing found in the FORGIVING Challenge Kids book is intended to be a substitute for professional psychological, psychiatric, or medical advice, diagnosis, or treatment.

Always seek the advice of your physician or other qualified mental health provider with any questions you may have regarding a medical condition or mental disorder. Never disregard professional medical advice or delay in seeking it because of something you have read in this book.

READY FOR THE NEXT CHALLENGE?

WWW.REDLETTERCHALLENGE.COM/CHURCH

WWW.BEINGCHALLENGE.COM/CHURCH

GET BULK PRICING + FREE STUFF:
SERMON MANUSCRIPTS
SMALL GROUP GUIDES + VIDEOS
GRAPHICS PACKAGE
KIDS CURRICULUM AND MORE!